TALES OF OLD HONG KONG

Treasures from the Fragrant Harbour

Derek Sandhaus

"Hongkong is an island in the Southern China Sea.
A colony as British as a British Isle can be.
The safest of all havens to be found in seven seas.
For ex-official patriots and Chinese refugees."

Shamus A'Rabbitt, China Coast Ballads, *1938*

Tales of Old Hong Kong

ISBN-13: 978-988-18667-2-1

Published by Earnshaw Books Ltd. (Hong Kong).

Acknowledgments

Creating a book like this is far from an exact science and involves sifting through hundreds of computer and paper documents, collecting nuggets and hastily scribbling notes along the way. I have tried to be as complete as possible in terms of recording sources and citations, but something could easily have slipped through the cracks. Should you find any item lacking a citation or incorrectly attributed, please let us so we can make the appropriate changes to future editions.We believe all items included are out of copyright or are used within the bounds of fair usage.

I received a great deal of help in putting this book together. I would like to thank (in no particular order) Graham Earnshaw, Frank Zheng, Andrew Chubb, Alice Polk, Catherine Mathes, Paul French, Gareth Powell, Iain Manley, Geoffrey Somers and Andrew Galbraith for their assistance along the way.

Derek Sandhaus

An Old Hong Kong Chronology

1278: Emperor Duanzong, last Song Emperor, flees to Hong Kong from the Mongol hordes, dies soon after.

1513: Portuguese explorer Jorge Álvares becomes the first European to visit Hong Kong.

1821: China outlaws opium imports to Canton and Macau. British merchants begin unloading their cargo at Hong Kong and surrounding islands.

1823: Lord Napier unsuccessfully attempts to dictate Chinese policy with gunboats at the Battle of Bogue Fort, dies shortly thereafter.

1839: All British merchants ordered to leave Canton and many seek refuge in Hong Kong.

1839-1942: The First Opium War.

1841, January: China and Britain discuss a demand for Hong Kong to be ceded to Britain, but the two sides fail to agree on terms.

1841, January 26: Sir J.J. Bremer takes possession of Hong Kong for the British Crown.

1842, August 29: Treaty of Nanking cedes Hong Kong to Britain.

1846: Race course opens at Happy Valley; Hong Kong Club opens as 'The Taipans' Club'.

1856-1860: Second Opium War.

1860, October 18: First Convention of Peking transfers the southern part of the Kowloon peninsula to Britain.

1868: Reclamation expands seafront creating land extension known as the Praya.

1869: Suez Canal opens, creating a boom in trade between Europe and Asia.

1888: Star Ferry and Peak Tramway begin service.

1890: First electric street lights; Praya expanded.

1894: Colony hit by major outbreak of bubonic plague, much of the Chinese city is destroyed in sanitation efforts.

1898, June 9: Second Convention of Peking transfers northern Kowloon and the "New Territories" to Britain on a 99-year lease.

1899: Small skirmishes between British soldiers and villagers take place as the New Territories are occupied.

1908: Opium divans outlawed, but not opium smoking.

1911: Kowloon-Canton Railway completed.

1918, 26 February: Fire at Happy Valley kills hundreds.

1941, December 25: Hong Kong falls to the Japanese Imperial Army.

1945, August 15: Japan surrenders and British administration resumes shortly thereafter.

1946-1950: Chinese Civil War, huge numbers of refugees arrive in Hong Kong.

1949, October 1: Establishment of the People's Republic of China opens the way for Hong Kong's emergence as one of Asia's premier ports and industrial centres.

Introduction

Hong Kong, occupied in 1841 by the British, and returned to China in 1997, has been through its history a land of golden opportunity unlike anywhere else. It has been, and remains, a dazzling crossroads of East meets West and an economic machine of unmatched precision. But looking at the 'Pearl of the Orient' today, you would never guess that its first century was marked by endless examples of British greed and incompetence compounded by a series of natural catastrophes. This book reflects on the colourful personalities and circumstance from the era that created, against all odds, this marvellous city.

Our story begins with the day the British opium smugglers were un-ceremoniously evicted from Canton in 1839. Hong Kong wasn't at the top of their list of alternatives. They would have been perfectly content to stay on the lovely little enclave of Macau, but the Portuguese, not wishing to sour relations with China, declined to let them do so. So the irritable drug merchants claimed Hong Kong for the Crown in 1841, a move that was met with fierce rebukes from Queen Victoria and Foreign Secretary Lord Palmerston, who declared it to be a "barren rock with hardly a house upon it".

In honour of their monarch, the settlement established on the north-ern harbour shore of Hong Kong

Island was called Victoria, a name that never gained any currency. For many years, the colony, planned as a prosperous trading hub, operated at a substantial loss. Impassioned calls rained down from Parliament in London for it to be abandoned, most famously in an 1847 report entitled "Hongkong, its position, prospects, character, and utter worthlessness in every point of view to England".

Nature's initial judgment was equally grim. The first summer of possession kicked off with a substantial landslide. Soon after the first buildings were erected, many were washed away by a typhoon that very nearly drowned the colony's founder, Captain Charles Elliot. Of the troops first stationed in what later, rather ironically, become known as Happy Valley, nearly all dropped dead of malaria. In the years that fol-

lowed, pestilence thrived and tropical storms relentlessly beat down upon the island, though not without allowing a window long enough for the occasional devastating fire to burn down large swaths of the city.

Unsurprisingly, these challenging conditions failed to attract the Empire's best and brightest. Many of those who came were either running from something or eager to keep moving. Old Hong Kong was where the world's washed-up often washed up, giving rise to the moniker FILTH - Failed in London? Try Hong Kong.

It was a most undesirable posting for British administrators – far from the luxurious courts of Europe, the mysteries of Peking and the thrills of India. Few stayed long enough to learn anything much about their Chinese subjects. English businessmen and adventurers came, some to

PENINSULA HOTEL

A la Carte Grill
(6th floor)

DINNER DANSANT DAILY

From 8.30 p.m.

(Sundays excepted)

ROOF GARDEN

TEA DANCE DAILY

From 4.30 p.m. to 6.30 p.m.

(Sundays excepted)

ADMISSION FIFTY CENTS
including Tea.

Dancing nightly

Admission $1 per head.

THE HONGKONG AND SHANGHAI HOTELS, LTD.

amass small fortunes before a quick exit, some to languish in colonial poverty. The Chinese who came were mostly coolies from over the border in Guangdong, who typically stayed only long enough to save some money before heading back to their ancestral villages. There were also quite a few criminals seeking asylum or refuge from imperial Chinese justice. Both groups were largely uneducated and presented a number of challenges to Hong Kong's colonial administrators.

The British merchant elite, the Taipans, lived in the cooler climes of Victoria Peak, while the Chinese and the poorer Europeans lived figuratively and literally below. The gross inequality felt on a daily basis between colonial and colonized was codified by the civil administration

and erupted on occasion in violent labour protests or rampant criminal activity.

Not all, however, moved on seeking greener pastures. Some forward-looking individuals, both foreign and Chinese, saw a bright future for the colony and staked their fortunes on it, opening businesses and laying down roots. And slowly but surely, the population and the shipping trade of Hong Kong grew to a respectable volume. Hardly the behemoth that was Shanghai, of course, but respectable nonetheless. Hong Kong became a unique melting pot including more than its fair share of wayward travellers, ruthless merchants, bloodthirsty pirates and opportunists of all nationalities; a thriving entrepôt of business and a most fascinating little pocket of the Far East.

And therein lies the secret of Hong Kong's success. Despite all of its faults, it presented fantastic

The first official seal of the Hong Kong Colony

opportunities to those from all walks of life. 'Chinamen' and 'foreign devils', criminals and missionaries, businessmen and coolies all came to Hong Kong seeking to improve their lot, and those bold and lucky enough to seize the opportunities presented to them grew rich beyond their wildest imaginings. As the colony prospered, so did its people.

With time, the once-inhospitable outpost became deserving of the sacrifices that had been made in its name, because Hong Kong's diverse community learned to work through their differences and forge lasting partnerships. When the Japanese invaded in late 1941, Hong Kong was a city worth fighting for. And when, four years after the war, the Mainland and its gem, Shanghai, fell to the Communists, Hong Kong was ready to pick up the slack and take centre stage.

This book recounts the ups and downs, the thrills and disappointments of the first hundred-odd years of the Hong Kong Colony. This is a journey back in time to the rollicking days of Taipans and typhoons, poisonings and plagues. In the words of visitors and residents, in pictures, newspaper clippings and through vivid anecdotes, it contains an assortment of tales that are by turn lively, comic, tragic and, hopefully, entertaining. The highlights, stereotypes and misconceptions are all given equal play.

The picture of Hong Kong that emerges is more atmospheric than academic. This is in no way an attempt to give a complete account of the territory's history. This book is a small window into the city's past, simply an introduction to the major players, famous landmarks and the most outrageous incidents. My hope is that you will enjoy discovering the past of this magnificent city as much as I have.

Derek Sandhaus
Shanghai
November 2009

'Victoria West and P. & O. Hong' by George Chinnery, 1851.

Approaching Hong Kong

In Seaports of the Far East, Allister Macmillan, 1925

Early morning mist, and the tops of faraway peaks visible high up — *mo ten lang* as the Chinese say — magnificently touching the sky; the face of every Chinese aboard alight with anticipation and the joy of home-coming; the early morning sea spotted as far as the vision extends — hundreds of little specks that turn out to be big fishing junks, with high poops and brown matting sails, out for the daily catch; little islands and great mountains looming up nearer.

Your ship is approaching Hongkong; in its turn, according to the variations of shipping statistics, first port of the British Empire, if not, of the world — "gateway" to southern China, a monument to British pluck and British enterprise. As you gaze, some of the little islands reveal themselves as lumps of China's mainland, brown and barren mostly, their forestry burned long years since in the cooking stoves of the small fishing villages huddled at the water's edge. You are reminded of the many centuries and the great population of China, four hundred millions no less, the low standard of living, the thrift and contentment, the contrasts of wealth and poverty — and musing so, you are recalled to the twentieth century by the lighthouses and the big guns, marking the entrance to latter-day Hongkong.

> "We occupy Hongkong, not with the object of colonising, but of using it from a commercial and military point of view."
> *Lord Edward Stanley, 14th Earl of Derby, 1840s*

The Bona Fide First Possessors

From Narrative of a Voyage round the World performed in H.M.S. Sulphur, 1836-1842 *by Sir Edward Belcher, 1843*

We landed on Monday the 25th January, 1841, at fifteen minutes past eight A.M., and being the *bona fide* first possessors, Her Majesty's health was drunk with three cheers on Possession Mount. On the 26th the squadron arrived; the marines were landed, the Union Jack hoisted on our post, and formal possession taken of the Island by Commodore Sir J.G. Bremer, accompanied by the other officer of the squadron, under a *feu-de-joie* from the marines, and the Royal salute from the ships of war.

Hong Kong harbor around the 1860s.

Never to be Relinquished

From An Aide-de-Camp's Recollections of Service in China *by Arthur Cunynghame, 1844*

It struck me at that time, and circumstances have since borne me out, that we should never again relinquish this little spot; for however adverse our government might be to any territorial aggrandizement, it seemed perfectly requisite for us to possess some portion of land, neighboring the continent, where our own laws should be enforced, free from the chicanery and grasping insolence of the mandarins, and which, in case of any future trouble, might act as a place of future refuge to our shipping, and a secure retreat to our authorities, until such a force should arrive as would compel the Chinese authorities to respect the laws of civilized nations.

10

First Glimpse

One of the first English-language accounts of Hong Kong as recalled in Narrative of a Journey to the Interior of China *by Clarke Abel of Lord Amherst's Embassy, 1818*
The inhabitants of the Lemma Islands who came off to us in their boats were of a light copper colour, and very athletic: they managed their well constructed bamboo vessels with great dexterity. In the evening the squadron weighed and stood for Hong-kong, one of the Ladrone Islands…As seen from the ship, this island was chiefly remarkable for its high conical mountains, rising in the centre, and for a beautiful cascade which rolled over a fine blue rock into the sea…Its scenery is composed of barren rocks, deep ravines, and mountain-torrents, but presents few characters of a very picturesque description. Of its inhabitants none were seen but some poor and weather-beaten fishermen, spreading their nets, and drying the produce of their toils on the rocks which supported their miserable mud-huts…Hong-kong sound is represented by my naval friends as affording admirable shelter for ships of any burden; but its description in this point of view does not fall within my province.

Green Island, 1925.

Pirates going ashore near Hong Kong, 1920s.

11

By Any Other Name

The British named the settlement Victoria after their queen, but the city was known almost from the start solely by the name of the island on which it sits - Hong Kong. The origins of the name Hong Kong remain mysterious and there are no shortage of theories. The two characters mean 'fragrant' ('heung' in Cantonese) and 'harbour' ('gong' in Cantonese). The fishing village on the south side of the island, known in English as Aberdeen, is called Little Hong Kong in Chinese (heung gong zhai). But there appear to be no Chinese records that refer to the island by the name Hong Kong prior to the British occupation. The name appears to refer to the body of water between Kowloon and Hong Kong rather than to the island itself. Regardless, Davis's explanation for the name, below, is clearly a linguistic misunderstanding.

The First Harbour

In "Hong Kong: An Urban Study" by R.H. Hughes in the Geographical Journal, *1951* Hong Kong (Heung Kong) was originally the name given by fishermen to the harbour of Aberdeen on the south side of the island; this attracted ships because of the stream of sweet water which entered the sea at Waterfall Bay nearby. Europeans later applied the name to the whole island and the main harbour.

The name *Hong-kong* is a provincial corruption of *Hoong-keang*, "the red torrent," from the colour of the soil through which the stream flows previous to its fall over the cliff.
John Francis Davis, 1841

Hong Kong, an island lying off the mouth of the Canton River, South China; was ceded to Britain in 1842; is hilly and unproductive, but is well watered and tolerably healthy; it owes its great importance as a commercial centre to its favourable position, its magnificent harbour, and to its having been made a free port and the head-quarters of the European banks; opium is the chief import, silk and tea the principal exports; Victoria, a handsome city on the N. side, is the capital, seat of the British governor, &c.

From The Nuttall Encyclopædia *Edited by Rev. James Wood, 1907*

The Pokfulam waterfall, on the south side of the island.

The island of HONGKONG or "Fragrant Stream" 香港, pronounced Hiang-Kiang in the Mandarin Language, derives its name from that of one of the small streams on the South side of the island, which, from being the first spot known to Europeans, gave its title to the whole colony.

The Treaty Ports of China and Japan, *1867*

Worthless

From the very beginning, the Hong Kong Colony had powerful and vocal opponents. Not only were the early settlers dying of tropical illnesses by the boatload, the administration of the outpost was costing the Empire a small fortune. The most outspoken early critic was Colonial Treasurer, Robert Montgomery Martin, who submitted a report on the island to Parliament in 1847 with a chapter entitled "Hongkong, its position, prospects, character, and utter worthlessness in every point of view to England". Twice in the 1840s, motions were put forward for the abandonment of Hong Kong, but luckily, they both failed and by 1855, the Colony became self-supporting in all but military expenditures.

Not a Shilling More

In R.M. Martin to Gov. Davis, "Report on the Island of Hong Kong", 1844
I have in vain sought for one valuable quality in Hong Kong. There are other good harbours around, and for 200 years we have not found the want of such. I can see no justification for the British Government spending one shilling on Hong Kong.

Central Hong Kong, 1870s.

"If it could have been foreseen, what the total expenses would amount to, and what limited advantages this place would possess for our trade, it would have been thought not worth while to occupy it."
Lord Grey,
British Secretary of
State, 1840s

Samshu

J.H. Holland, The Bulletin of Miscellaneous Information, *1912*

"Samshu" is distilled from rice, in Hong Kong, where the spirit forms the basis of several beverages prepared by flavouring with plums, oranges and other fruits… The spirit possesses a peculiar pungent and disagreeable odour, which makes it unsuitable for certain purposes, but it is less pungent when the husk is removed before fermentation.

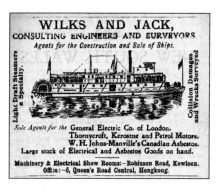

Pick your Poison

From Travels in the Far East *by Ellen Mary Hayes Peck, 1909*

The Hong-Kong Hotel is situated in the business centre; although under English management, the service was entirely Chinese, and at luncheon we were confronted by an array of waiters with braids around their heads and wearing long blue garments made like aprons; the ensemble was indeed most depressing. The menu presented a curious feature, the courses being numbered, and you were expected to point to the number, but woe to any one who wished an egg boiled four minutes or a piece of rare roast!

HONG KONG HOTEL

HONG KONG, CHINA

"These colonial women drink less during the evenings than mornings; the men seldom drink during the mornings, but the evenings are very moist."
John Stuart Thomson,
The Chinese, *1909*

Notable Hongs

Butterfield and Swire . . . . Est. 1867 in Shanghai
David Sassoon, Sons and Co. . . . . Est. 1832 in Bombay
Dent & Co. . . . . Est. 1824 in Canton
Dodwell's (orig. W.R. Adamson & Co.) . . . . Est. 1852 in Shanghai
Gilman and Bowman . . . . Est. 1840 in Canton
Hong Kong and Whampoa Dock Co. ... Est. 1863 by Lepraik and Sutherland
Hong Kong Electric . . . . Est. 1890 by Chater et al
Hong Kong Land . . . . Est. 1889 by Chater and J. Keswick
Hongkong and Shanghai Banking Corp. . . . . Est. 1865 by Sutherland
Jardine, Matheson and Co. . . . . Est. 1832 in Canton
Russell & Co. . . . . Est. 1824 in Canton

> HONG. Mercantile
> houses in China,
> with convenient
> warehouses
> adjoining. Also,
> a society of the
> principal merchants
> of the place.
> *W.H. Smyth's*
> Sailor's Word-Book,
> *1867*

Advantage Chinaman

In Trade and Travel in the Far East *by G.F. Davidson, 1846*

A decisive proof of the eligibility of Hong Kong as a place of trade, and of its importance in the eyes of the Chinese themselves, is afforded by the immense sums paid by some of them for ground on which to build *Hongs*, where they can deposit their goods with safety, beyond the reach of their grasping Mandarins. This advantage to a China-man is something so new, and so far beyond any thing he ever dreamed of enjoying, that I conceive the benefits likely to accrue from it to Hong Kong to be incalculable.

The Colony that 'Just Hums'

From The Peoples and Politics of the Far East *by Henry Norman, 1895*

When you land in the city of Victoria (it is strange, by the way, that almost everybody at home and half the visitors there are ignorant that "Victoria" is the name of the city and "Hongkong" of the island), the inevitable 'ricksha carries you through a couple of streets, far from being beautiful or well-managed, but you forget this in the rush of life about you. Messengers jostle you, 'rickshas run over your toes, chair-poles dig you in the ribs. The hotel clerk smiles politely as he informs you that there has not been a vacant room for a month. Later on your fellow-passengers envy you the little rabbit-hole of a bedroom you have secured at the top of the Club. When you come down again into the hall you find it crowded with brokers of many nationalities, making notes, laughing, whispering, drinking, but all just as busy as they can be. The Stock Exchange of Hongkong was the gutter, the local Rialto extending from the Club for about a hundred yards down the Queen's road, and it was filled with Britishers, Germans, Anglo-Indians, Chinese from Canton, Armenians from Calcutta, Parsees from Bombay, and Jews from Baghdad, and with that peculiar contingent known as the "black brigade," recognizable by the physiognomy of Palestine and the accent of Spitalfields. And on the Club walls and tables are a dozen printed "Expresses," timed with the minute at which they were issued, and the mail and shipping noon and afternoon "extras" of the daily papers, announcing the arrival and departures of steamers, the distribution of cargoes, the sales by auction, and all the multitudinous movements of a great commercial machine running at high pressure. For, to apply to the Far East the nomenclature of the Far West, this colony "just hums" all the time.

Bonham Strand, 1920s.

17

Opium Haven

From China *by W.H. Medhurst, 1838*

Never was a weak and pusillanimous government more violently roused than the Chinese authorities appear to be, on the subject of the illicit traffic in opium. The native dealers in the drug, are obliged to flee into holes and corners, the foreign opium-merchants have been required to leave Canton; the quiet anchorage of the receiving ships, at Kap-sing-moon, has been broken up, and the smugglers obliged to retreat to Hong-kong bay.

"The island of Hongkong will probably become the favourite resort of the s mugglers and debauchees of that quarter of the globe."
A high British official, 1841

No Cause for Indignation

From Trade and Travel in the Far East *by G.F. Davidson, 1846*

As a convenient and safe *dépôt* for opium, (a trade, in my opinion, quite as legitimate and honourable as that in brandy, gin, and other spirits,) Hong Kong is admirably situated: the purchaser from the western ports, as well as from the northeastern, finds the distance he has to travel moderate, and, on his arrival, has no one to dread, no Mandarin daring to shew his face on shore…I confess I see no reason for the clamorous indignation with which this traffic has of late been assailed by European moralists… The Chinese are just as capable of taking care of themselves as their would-be guardians are; and as for their morals, many of them lead lives that might be copied with advantage to themselves and families, by thousands of gin-drinking Englishmen.

Junks in Hong Kong harbor around 1870.

Refuge of the Oppressed

From Europe in China *by E.J. Eitel, 1895*
Ever since the first dawning of its known history, Hongkong was the refuge of the oppressed from among the nations. The Hakkas ill-treated by the Puntis, the Puntis Tie-chius and Tan-ka people weary of the yoke of mandarinism, as well as the Chinese Emperor fleeing before the ruthless Tartar invaders, the industrious Chinese settler as well as the roving pirate, and finally the British merchant, self-exiled from Europe finding his personal and national self-respect trampled underfoot by Manchu-Chinese tyrants–all turned, with hesitating reluctance but impelled by resistless fate, to the island of Hongkong as the haven of refuge, the home of the free.

Yaumatei taiphoon shelter with Hong Kong in the background, 1910.

"Chinese authorities regard British law as a means whereby their own criminals escape punishment, as many of them undoubtedly do."
Henry Norman, The Peoples and Politics of the Far East, *1895*

"When the colony of Hong Kong was first established in 1842, it was forthwith invaded by brothel keepers and prostitutes from the adjoining districts of the mainland of China, who brought with them the national Chinese system of prostitution, and have ever since labored to carry it into effect in all its details."
An Imperial Maritime Customs Service Officer, 1879

19

Happy Valley

Happy Valley was the first proposed location for the settlement, but the swampy flatlands proved to be a malarial death trap with bad *Feng Shui*, so the town was established further along the shore to the west. It was first called Belcher Valley, after an unfortunately named administrator, but later it took on the rather ironic, upbeat name it bears today. The valley, which killed many of the unfortunate British soldiers charged with draining it, later became the site of English, Catholic, Parsee, Muslim and Jewish cemeteries.

Most famously, Happy Valley is the home to Hong Kong's first race course, which opened after the draining of the swamp in 1846. It is a difficult course with sharp turns and, in the early years, suffered from occasional flooding and the occasional stray dog causing trouble on the track. The races were by far the most popular social event on the island and the scene of many petty squabbles between merchants and officials. The track's popularity and relative remoteness from downtown also made Happy Valley the perfect home for many a mistress. And in this one regard at least, it lived up to its name.

Happy Valley, late 19th century.

White Man's Grave

From China in Transformation *by Archibald R. Colquhoun, 1898*
In the early period of our possession the climate of the lower valleys was so bad that "abandon hope" might have been written up over the barrack gateway. Not ten men of the 59th Regiment remained of those who eight years before had landed there, and the place acquired the name of "The White Man's Grave."

The Happy Valley race course, early 1900s.

A Most Pleasant Social Meeting

From A Voyage in the 'Sunbeam' *by Annie Allnut Brassey, 1881*
We were puzzled to imagine where, on this rocky, hilly island, there could possibly be found a piece of ground flat enough for a race-course. But the mystery was solved when we reached a lovely little valley, about two miles from the town, where we found a very fair course…The grand stand is a picturesque object, with its thatched roof, verandahs, and sun-blinds. The interior, too, looks comfortably arranged, and certainly contains the most luxurious basket-chairs one could possibly desire. There are a lawn and a paddock attached, and very good temporary stables, over many of which are private stands and tiffin-rooms…Everybody knows everybody, and it seems to be altogether a most pleasant social meeting.

21

Karl Gützlaff

A Man of God and friend of opium smugglers, the Pomeranian Reverend Karl "Charles" Friedrich August Gützlaff was a most colorful addition to old Hong Kong. A natural linguist, he is best known for his work as an interpreter, particularly at the Treaty of Nanking talks in 1842, where a drunken Manchu official gave him a sloppy kiss. He also helped to complete a translation of the bible into Chinese, which later inspired Taiping Rebellion leader Hong Xiuquan to decide he was the younger brother of Jesus. Later scholars have questioned his Chinese ability, but until 1844 he was the Colony's only official translator, its Chinese affairs minister, and a favorite of the opium merchants.

As the French Consul of Macau noted, Gützlaff was 'a man of considerable inventiveness, who has always sought to enrich himself'. He married three times in the Orient, amassing a small fortune in inheritance.

But as one of the Far East's first protestant missionaries, he also found some time to preach the gospel to the heathens. Adopting native dress and a queue (ponytail), he opened the first school for Chinese missionaries. He printed and distributed large numbers of Chinese bibles and thought he was doing quite well until he realized that his 'missionaries' were in league with the printers and spending most of the profits on opium. It caused a great scandal and Gützlaff died shortly thereafter in 1851, at only 48 years old.

"I would give a thousand dollars for three days with Gutzlaff."

Captain James Innes, around 1832

Old Men in Yellow

From Around the World in 80 Days *by Jules Verne, 1874*

Passepartout wandered, with his hands in his pockets, towards the Victoria port, gazing as he went at the curious palanquins and other modes of conveyance, and the groups of Chinese, Japanese, and Europeans who passed to and fro in the streets. Hong Kong seemed to him not unlike Bombay, Calcutta, and Singapore, since, like them, it betrayed everywhere the evidence of English supremacy. At the Victoria port he found a confused mass of ships of all nations: English, French, American, and Dutch, men-of-war and trading vessels, Japanese and Chinese junks, sempas, tankas, and flower-boats, which formed so many floating parterres. Passepartout noticed in the crowd a number of the natives who seemed very old and were dressed in yellow. On going into a barber's to get shaved he learned that these ancient men were all at least eighty years old, at which age they are permitted to wear yellow, which is the Imperial colour. Passepartout, without exactly knowing why, thought this very funny.

The Peak Tram

The summer heat in Hong Kong drove many of its more affluent residents up the Peak, but for decades the journey to and from the top was neither fast nor convenient, requiring a team of coolies with sedan chairs. All this changed in 1888, when Governor Des Voeux unveiled a funicular railway that could climb the Peak in less than ten minutes. Des Voeux and subsequent governors would use the Peak Tram, as it was called, to travel between Government House and Mountain Lodge (their summer residence) with a special seat bearing the inscription 'This seat is reserved for his Excellency The Governor'. It was the height of modern engineering at the time of its construction and, to this day, has never had an accident.

Heard in the Tram

From John Chinaman at Home *by Rev. E.J. Hardy, 1905*
The journey occupies only seven minutes, but in less time than this a reputation may be slain, and "Heard in the tram" is the authority for many a lie. Those who travel up and down the tram two or three or four times a day get very tired of each other. One can meet a person twice a day with breezy enthusiasm, but the third time the smile of recognition is sickly, and the fourth time there is an incipient scowl. To those not accustomed to the tram the houses on either side look as if they were toppling over. Newcomers hold on to their seat and murmur, "Oh my!"

Kennedy Road, 1900.

The Modern Chinese Girl

From North of Singapore, *by Carveth Wells, 1940*

The dance hour at tea or cocktail time in the Hongkong Hotel presents one of the most fascinating scenes in the Far East – that is, if you are interested in pretty Chinese girls. Unbecoming trousers have given way to the slit skirt, which seems to have been purposely designed to show off the charming legs of Chinese women. The modern Chinese girl, with Madame Chiang Kai-shek as an example, looks forward to a career that only liberty and complete freedom can offer her.

> "Do not be afraid of my falling in love with the "little feet" and "long hair" of the Chinese ladies. There is very little attraction about them for me, though they are superior to the men in every respect, especially in good looks."
>
> *B.L. Ball*, Rambles in Eastern Asia, *1856*

Hong Kong Pearls

From "Hongkong Sing Song" in Shamus A'Rabbitt's China Coast Ballads, *1938*

Hongkong is an island in
The Southern China Sea
Where dusky maidens smile and
The sing song girls are free.

The sing song girls in China are
A-beckoning to me
From Hongkong and Eastern Asia
From tropic isles and sea.

Hongkong girls are Hongkong pearls
As dusky as can be
For Hongkong is an island in
The Southern China Sea.

The Freest Port in the East

One of the principle reasons for Hong Kong's eventual success was its status as a 'Free Port', that is, a port where merchants of any nation could store their goods without paying customs duties. As such, it became an ideal location for the many goods sailing in and out of China, particularly after the 1869 opening of the Suez Canal and the improving quality of steam engines considerably shortened the journey from Europe. Before long, Hong Kong became the Far East's most important entrepôt, or storehouse for goods in transit.

Asia's Clearing House

Memorandum on the Trade of Hong Kong from American Council of Pacific Relations, *1934*

A closer examination of the situation in Hongkong shows that local industries are much more a by-product of Hongkong's economic life than a cause. In fact they are comparatively unimportant. The chief function of the port is to act as a clearing house for goods destined for other regions. This is clearly shown, though not specifically pointed out, in the foreign trade statistics of the Colony, which indicate that between 73 and 80 per cent (in 1922, over 90 per cent) of Hongkong's imports are reshipped to other regions.

> "Hong Kong is a free port, and, in my opinion, ought never to be otherwise than free. Let its harbour be a refuge for the shipping of all nations, and its stores will then be filled with their goods."
>
> *G.F. Davidson,* Trade and Travel in the Far East, *1846*

The Monotony of Life

Laurence Oliphant, private secretary to Lord Elgin, 1862
The charms of the Club or the excitement of a game of billiards failed to tempt us. Hong-Kong boasts of only two walks for the conscientious valetudinarian – one along the sea-shore to the right, and the other to the left of the settlement: then there is a scramble to the top of Victoria Peak at the back of it, but this achievement involves an early start, and a probable attack of fever. The monotony of life is varied by this malady alternating with boils or dysentery; so that the proverbial hospitality of the merchants at Hong-Kong can only be exercised under very adverse influences. It was not difficult to account for a certain depression of spirits and tone of general irritability, which seemed to pervade the community. A large bachelor's dinner was the extreme limit of gaiety.

A Whirl

Isabella Bird, The Golden Chersonese and the Way Thither, *1883*
Victoria is, or should be, well known, so I will not describe its cliques, its boundless hospitalities, its extravagances in living, its quarrels, its gayeties, its picnics, balls, regattas, races, dinner parties, lawn tennis parties, amateur theatricals, afternoon teas, and all its other modes of creating a whirl which passes for pleasure or occupation.

Hong-Kong

From "The Song of the Cities" in Rudyard Kipling's The Seven Seas, *1897*
Hail, Mother! Hold me fast; my Praya sleeps
Under innumerable keels to-day.
Yet guard (and landward) or to-morrow sweeps
Thy warships down the bay.

The Princely Hong

The name of Jardine, Matheson & Co. is inseparable from that of Hong Kong. Founded in 1832 by Dr. William Jardine, surgeon for the British East India Company turned opium trader, and fellow Scotsman James Matheson, the firm quickly became a dominant force in Canton opium trade, controlling as much as a third of total volume within a few years. Matheson was the more refined partner, oversaw the firm's administration and organization, and supposedly owned the only piano in Asia. Jardine, dubbed 'Old Iron-headed Rat' by the Chinese after shrugging off a vicious club blow to the head, was the older and more fearsome one. He kept only one chair in his office, his own, and made all visitors state their business briefly while standing. His departure from Canton in 1839 was prematurely celebrated by Chinese officials, who promptly seized British opium stores. Jardine, in turn, went off to Whitehall to persuade Foreign Secretary Palmerstone to protect his firm's trade with gunboats. So was launched the First Opium War and, of course, Hong Kong, where a Jardine Matheson opium godown (warehouse) was the first permanent building erected.

Jardine, now a member of Parliament, died in 1843 and Matheson sailed for London to fill his partner's now-vacant seat. Jardine, Matheson & Co. stopped selling opium in the 1870s, but their legacy in Hong Kong and the Far East endured. Officially, Scottish ancestry and kinship were not required for success in the firm, but it certainly helped and most future Taipans would come from the Keswick family, descended from William Jardine's sister. Always the most prestigious firm in Hong Kong, it became known as the 'Princely Hong', and also had the respect of Hong Kong's Chinese (who knew it as 'Ewo' or 'pleasant harmony'), employing many locals and helping several, like compradore (Chinese manager) Robert Ho Tung, amass significant fortunes. Even today, when most of the old Hongs have long since vanished, Jardines remains.

Jardine and Matheson's godowns (warehouses) and offices, 1855.

The Biggest Taipan

Rudyard Kipling in From Sea to Sea, *1899*
He was the biggest *Taipan* on the island, and
quite the nicest . . . To him, said I: —
"O *Taipan*, I am a poor person from
Calcutta, and the liveliness of your place
astounds me. How is it that every one smells
of money; whence come your municipal
improvements; and why are the White Men so
restless?"

Dr. William Jardine

"The Gazelle was unnecessarily
delayed at Hong Kong in
consequence of Captain Crocker's
repugnance to receiving opium
on the Sabbath. We have every
respect for persons entertaining
strict religious principles, but we
fear that very godly people are not
suited for the drug trade. Perhaps
it would be better that the Captain
should resign."

Sir James Matheson

The Heart of the Colony

From Twentieth Century Impressions of Hongkong, Shanghai, and other Treaty
Ports of China *edited by Arnold Wright, 1908*
With all that concerns the welfare of the Colony of Hongkong those connected
with Jardine, Matheson & Co. have ever been closely identified. Streets bear the
name of long-departed partners, the City Hall was built mainly owing to the
public-spirited generosity of Sir Robert Jardine, while on the Legislative and
Executive Councils it has been seldom indeed that the firm's representative
has not held a seat.

Bandits

Though the pirates of Hong Kong got more international attention, their landlubbing counterparts were no less active in Hong Kong's rough and tumble early years. Most criminal activity came in the form of barroom brawls and petty theft, often escalating into violence and murder. In comparison to the brutal punishments and hardly impartial trials they could expect on the Mainland, the British legal system offered a softer alternative and, for some, a carte blanche to run amuck. This early wave of criminality died down by the late 19th century, but organized crime and carefully orchestrated heists were still a major threat in later years.

> "Hongkong is getting into a dreadfully unsafe state…Many ladies of Hong Kong always carry a loaded revolver with them which they can fire six times, and others carry "Penang lawyers," or sticks, or life-preservers."
>
> *Mrs. James Legge, c1859*

Target Practice

From the letters of Lord Elgin, British Commander during the Second Opium War, 1856

Hong-kong. — December 5th. — When I went out to walk with Oliphant, I was informed by a person I met in a very public walk just out of the town, that a man had been robbed very near where we were. I met the person immediately afterwards. He was rather a mesquin-looking Portuguese, and he said that three Chinamen had rushed upon him, knocked him down, thrown a quantity of sand into his eyes, and carried off his watch. This sort of affair is not uncommon. I have bought a revolver, and am beginning to practice pistol-shooting.

Sikh policemen with a prisoner in stocks.

Chinese Population

1841: 4,350 (island only)
1865: 121,497
1895: 237,670
1921: 625,166
1938: over 1 million
1950: 2.2 million

Sanctuary

Hong Kong was intended to be a place where free trade could thrive under the British flag. Predictably, Chinese people also flocked there to seek the Crown's protection. Initially, many were transients of the coolie and criminal variety. Later, most were just looking for stability.

Hong Kong's first hundred years were tumultuous ones for China. Shortly after possession, the Taiping Rebellion (1850-64) raged across south China. In 1912, the Qing Dynasty fell, then came the Warlord Era (1916-28), the Sino-Japanese War (1937-45) and the Chinese Civil War (1946-49). The colony was uneventful by comparison, and the numbers reflect that: the population grew from less than 5,000 Chinese in 1841 to over 2 million by 1950.

Political refugees came to Hong Kong in droves, too. There, they could avoid their enemies and publish freely. Qing-era reformer Kang You-wei fled to Hong Kong in 1900, rather than submit to 'death by a thousand cuts'. The 'Father of Modern China', Sun Yat-sen, staged his first rebellion while based in Hong Kong in 1895 (and couldn't return for years because of it). Many a Chinese warlord also spent time there, as did communists like Zhou Enlai and Deng Xiaoping. The political landscape of China today would look very different if not for the haven that was Hong Kong.

Wellington Street, 1880s.

"The worst thing about the Chinese is that there are so many of them. They get on your nerves. No matter what you are doing, you feel that you are being overlooked. The celestial part of Hong Kong is more crowded than any place except a herring-barrel, and there are always more people wanting to come in."

Rev. E.J. Hardy, 1905

31

In the Native Quarter

From Hongkong China *from the U.S. Bureau of Navigation's U.S. Navy Ports of the World series, 1921*

Proceeding into the native quarter, the visitor finds himself in a district as crowded as Manhattan and with a people as varied in nationality as those in the East Side of New York City. The predominant race, of course, is Chinese, but there are East Indians, Hindoos, South Sea Islanders, and other transplanted peoples whose presence heightens the cosmopolitan effect apparent even in the poorest sections of Hongkong...There are narrow streets and dark, foul alleys, and damp cellars; dingy houses, whose frames look as if they had lived their lives and were preparing quietly to collapse; slant-eyed coolies in breech clouts, toiling beneath their loads of merchandise or provender; mandarins in heavily embroidered robes that breathe a faint aroma of oriental perfumes; Chinese merchants in round black caps and satin slippers, chattering with their customers; pale yellow students with composed features and oily hair; long strips of paper hanging in front of the shops and stores inscribed with characters in the Chinese language.

A little farther on we see a stout person with pigtail coiled around his head walk across the narrow sidewalk, lift himself into a jinrikisha and speak a word of command to the diminutive human beast of burden who immediately starts up the crowded street, hauling the stout person at a good rate of speed.

In the dirt of the street sits a beggar with sunken eyes and talons for fingers, and whose wrinkled skin resembles saffron colored parchment. The beggar lifts his voice in a singsong whine for alms – and a "cash" or Chinese coin of little value is gratefully received with a word of blessing. If the beggar goes without alms he usually does not abuse the passers-by, nor hurl curses at them, as does the beggar of other nations, but instead he sits dreaming for a while and with a far-away look in his sunken eyes, only coming to himself with a start when the dull ache of hunger in his stomach reminds him that life still remains in

his ancient body.

On the other side of the street a schoolgirl in silk blouse and trousers, with mouselike feet and shining hair, pilots a small person of five or six — evidently her brother — through the ebb and flow of traffic. They jabber excitedly and seem to find a great deal of interest in the quaint signs along the way. Following them is a small dog of questionable breed who stops a moment to fight the cloud of fleas swarming over him and snarls and yelps impatiently at the persistence of the insects.

There is a great uproar at the corner. A coolie has dropped a sack of rice and the white kernels lie strewn about in the water and mud, while the owner of the grain, greatly angered and with contorted face, is belaboring the coolie with a club. Two native policemen interfere and lead the angry one and the coolie away. The angry one is expostulating in his singsong voice, while the coolie is busily engaged in rubbing his hurts.

Upon turning a corner the odor of fish fills the nostrils and there, in long rows of stalls, are piled thousands of mackerel, trout, perch, and other specimens of the innumerable finny tribes which swarm in the waters around Hongkong. Some of the fish are fresh, but life in some of them, undoubtedly, has been extinct a long time. Both varieties are eagerly purchased by the Chinese who eat them with rice. The larger fish are sought by the wealthy classes, while tiny fish no larger than a small coin are bought by the poorest of the poor who consider them quite delectable. Field rats are also eaten by the natives, and this practice has given rise to the belief that Chinese are great eaters of common gray rats. Such a belief is really a libel on the Chinese — for the gray rats are as different from the field rats of China as the dogfish is from the succulent rainbow trout — and a respectable Chinaman would no sooner think of eating a common gray rat than an American would think of doing likewise.

33

Boxing Centre of the Far East

"Pugilism in China", New York Times, Dec. 31, 1911

Hongkong is the centre of boxing in the Far East. Large sums are wagered on the outcomes of the battles, and any fighter who shows merit can get backing for almost any amount…The best fight of recent date at the City Hall was the featherweight championship of the Orient between Iron Bux, holder of the title, and Private Potter of the marines, challenger. Many bets were placed, all favoring Bux because of the form he had displayed in former bouts. Potter, however, won handily on points in a fifteen-round bout, which was full of fast work from start to finish.

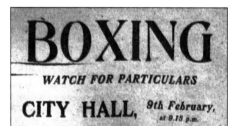

There was an old man of Hong Kong,
Who never did anything wrong;
He lay on his back, with his head in a sack,
That innocuous old man of Hong Kong.

From The Best Nonsense Verse, *1872*

Wharves of the Hongkong and Kowloon Wharf and Godown Co., 1925.

34

Stamping and Thrumming

"Around-the-World Letters" by Charlotte Ehrlicher in the American Journal of Nursing, *1913*

That night we went to the theatre. I never saw such a crowded house, nor such a study in black and white, for we sat on the stage looking right into this sea of smooth white faces, shining black hair and plain black garments. Men, women, and children were smoking. There is no scenery, only a table with a red cover and two or three chairs. The exaggerated gestures, aided by the Chinese imagination, convey the idea of a man mounting and riding away. The girl climbs on the table and gets down on the other side, she has disappeared over the mountain. The stabbed man smears himself with red right before your eyes, and then walks off-dead. There are no actresses, men take the women's parts, and are paid the highest salaries. I never heard such falsetto shrieks, such stamping and shouting. It was deafening – a Chinese edition of "Elektra." The musicians sit in the centre of the stage at the back, and keep up an incessant thrumming through the whole performance, indicating the play of human passions with a varying volume of sound. To us it was most grotesque, but the audience sat with tears in their eyes, or laughter, and their attitudes were as tense as our audiences are at an Ibsen play.

Cantonese opera actors around 1910.

"The Chinese do not appreciate our music any more than we do theirs. A Chinese, who was listening to the military band playing in Hongkong, was asked his opinion of it, and he said the music lacked harmony."

J. Dyer Ball,
Things Chinese,
1903

Hard to Swallow

In the early years of Hong Kong, many Chinese bitterly resented their uninvited British neighbours and made no attempts to hide it. Within a month of the British Navy landing in Hong Kong, there were already rumours circulating about Chinese attempts to poison their drinking water. About a decade later, tensions still running high, a Chinese cook was arrested for attempting to poison a group of 25 artillery officers.

The most famous poisoning case involved someone putting arsenic in the bread at a popular Hong Kong bakery on January 15, 1857. Several foreign residents were poisoned, but the bungling would-be assassin put such a large amount of poison in the dough that not one person was able to keep the tainted pastries down. The chief Chinese baker A-lum was taken into custody, but he was ultimately acquitted because he and his family were also poisoned. Many suspected the involvement of meddling Chinese officials in Canton, specifically Ye Mingchen, and this event undoubtedly helped foment the outrage and paranoia that would begin the Second Opium War.

The Wanchi Steam Bakery, seen here in the 1860, was established shortly after the 1857 poisonings.

Don't Drink the Water

"Notice to the Chinese People against Poisoning the Water." Hong Kong, *Sept. 2, 1839*

A Placard, said to be posted on shore at Hong Kong, to the following effect, has this day been exhibited to Elliot, the English Superintendent: Poison has been put into this water, which will destroy the bowels if it be drunk. Let none of our people take it to drink… He knows that the higher officers are incapable of issuing such shameful papers, and that they are the work of low and designing men. Elliot now exhorts all the good and peaceable natives of the neighbourhood not to lend themselves to such practices, so sure to draw down the just wrath of the great Emperor, and to lead to conflict with the foreign men.

Cantonese Mischief

From The Uncollected Writings of Thomas de Quincey (Vol. 2), *January 1859*
No sympathy with our horror of secret murders by poison, under the shelter of household opportunities, must be counted on from the emperor, for he has himself largely encouraged, rewarded, and decorated these claims on his public bounty. The more necessary that such nests of crime as Canton, and such suggestors of crime as Yeh, should be thoroughly disarmed…it is evident enough that the colonial head-quarters at Hong-Kong must in future keep up a *permanent* military establishment; and since any danger threatening this colony must be kindled and fed chiefly in Canton, why not make this large city, sole focus as it is of all mischief to us, and not a hundred miles distant from the little island, the main barrack of the armed force?

Everything in its Place

From English Life in China *by Major Henry Knollys, 1885*

Among the natural productions of the country, the very best and foremost is the race of Chinese servants, or 'boys' as they are invariably called, whether their age be sixteen or sixty: very quick in learning their business, sharp all round, clean, attentive, and for the most part singularly honest, so far that they will suffer no one but themselves to pilfer their masters, and that their own depredations are limited to certain recognised 'squeezing' or extortion in commission. Each one makes the general and particular character of his master his special study sometimes to a very amusing extent. The first day I engaged my 'boy,' I had carelessly tossed my hat into one corner of the room, gloves on the bed, a stump of pencil at an acute angle with one corner of the mantelpiece, and a pipe at the other corner. For many successive days I found hat, gloves, stump of pencil and pipe carefully deposited in exactly the same spot and at precisely the same angle.

It Ain't Chinese

From Susan Clegg and a Man in the House *by Anne Warner, 1907*

Well, the book begins very mild an' pleasant with Hongkong an' it ends with the Philippine accounts. Seems Hongkong ain't Chinese for all it's named that an' growed there—it's English—an' as for the Philippines there's eight millions of 'em, not countin' the wild ones as they can't catch to count an' ask questions.

38

"The "Pidjun English" is revolting, and the most dignified persons demean themselves by speaking it. The word "pidjun" appears to refer generally to business. "My pidjun" is undoubtedly "my work." How the whole English-speaking community, without distinction of rank, has come to communicate with the Chinese in this baby talk is extraordinary."
Isabella Bird, The Golden Chersonese and the Way Thither, *1883*

SOLE AGENTS FOR KELVIN MOTORS.
W. S. BAILEY & CO., LTD.
ENGINEERS, SHIPBUILDERS AND REPAIRERS.
Designers and Builders of Fast Steam and Motor Vessels Tugs, Yachts, Launches and Lighters in Steel or Wood; Castings and Forgings Steel Buildings and Roofings.
LAND AND MARINE REPAIRS AND SUPPLIES.

S.S. "HAI NING," 15.6 KNOTS.
Reconstructed by W.S BAILEY & Coⁿ Ltd.

A Miserable Substitute

From English Life in China *by Major Henry Knollys, 1885*
It is exceedingly vexatious to be compelled to deal with that miserable substitute Pidgin English not, remember, the imperfect broken jargon of foreigners, but a hybrid gibberish interspersed with a variety of bastard Chinese or Portuguese terms...the basis of which is the conversion of every r into an l, adding final vowels to each word and the constant use of certain argot expressions. An 'American' is rendered 'Mellican man'; 'savvy' means ' to know,' from the Portuguese 'sabe.' 'Speak' is 'talkee'; 'piece' 'piecee'; exalted 'rank' or 'excellent,' 'number one'; 'do you understand' and 'that will answer the purpose' are both translated 'can do.'

Pirates!

Old Hong Kong was infested with pirates. One would be tempted to think that the British commerce had attracted the swashbucklers, but in actuality Chinese pirates used the island as a base as far back as the Yuan Dynasty (1271-1368). Hong Kong was, after all, part of the island group known as the Ladrones, Spanish for 'Thieves'. Many Hong Kong pirates also became international celebrities, like the American Eli Boggs, and pirate queen La Choi San, immortalized in Aleko Lilius' *I Sailed with Chinese Pirates.*

With so many remote coves and tiny islands nearby, like long-time pirate favourite Bias Bay, there were no shortage of hiding places for booty and hideaways from the authorities. Piracy was often a family business, with fleets sometimes numbering in the hundreds of junks passed down from a pirate chief to his progeny. It was a dangerous business, rife with murder and kidnapping, but a most profitable one for those able to avoid the gallows.

In the early years, Hong Kong pirates would, in the guise of fishermen, ambush ships in narrow channels near the island. Weapons of choice included swords, axes, pistols and bludgeoning objects of all kinds. Worst of all was the dreaded stink pot, a clay pot filled with all things foul (rotten meat and eggs, piss, sulphur) and sometimes gunpowder, so horrible that it could clear the deck of a ship, create noxious stink clouds and even induce surrender.

As time went on and Her Majesty's Navy's attempts to suppress their activities proved mostly futile, the pirates grew bolder and more cunning. Pirates had originally opted to target Chinese fishermen and traders, but by the late 19th century began staging complex attacks on European steamers. Stowed away or pretending to be passengers, the pirates would rush the deck, murder the guards and make away with the valuables on board. Piracy became big business, taking in hundreds of thousands of dollars annually by the 1920s, and continued to terrorize the China coast well into the 20th century.

No Mercy

From The Peoples and Politics of the Far East *by Henry Norman, 1895*

In spite of all denials, piracy is still rife in the waters around Hongkong. Chinese junks are the constant victims, and the eyes of the Colony were opened in 1890 by the piracy of the British steamer *Namoa,* which was seized by her Chinese passengers, two of her officers and a number of her crew shot, the remaining officers and European passengers imprisoned in the cabin, like another "Black Hole," for eight hours, the captain dying there, the loot transferred to six junks which came alongside at a signal, and then abandoned, after the windlass had been broken, the fires drawn, the lifeboats stove in, and the sidelights thrown overboard.

The son of pirate queen Lai Choi San, late 1920s.

Say, Old Chap, Are You a Pirate?

Adventure journalist Aleko E. Lilius describes his quest to meet Hong Kong pirates in I Sailed with Chinese Pirates, *1930*

The police did not want to help me. And one does not go along the streets of Hong-Kong asking every Chinese one meets: "Say, old chap, are you a pirate? If so, please tell me all about it." But luck was with me.

Walking one day along the steep, hilly streets, and looking into curio shop windows, I noticed a man leaning against a casement. His right ear was missing. Where it should have been there was a great black hole in his skull. Putting aside all thought of manners, I pointed, tourist-like, at the place where his ear should have been, and asked him what had happened to it. He smiled broadly.

"Chinee pilates choppee off ear. Send him by my blother. He! He! He!"

"You don't say! Tell me all about it!"

Marital Bliss

Mrs. James Legge in James Legge Missionary and Scholar, *1905*

Yesterday we were kept in continual uproar by a Chinese wedding, which takes place in the neighborhood oftener than we desire. Through the night previous and on the wedding-day there are tremendous explosions of crackers. A grand Chinese chair is brought for the bride, another for the mother, and also lanterns and streamers. A crowd collects, and the greatest excitement prevails, in the midst of which, after explosions of crackers, a company dressed as priests, clad in scarlet, appears. But what most strikes you is the rudeness of the ceremony. These mock priests, clad in scarlet, wear trousers which may be denominated as filthy, and no shoes or stockings. They make a clatter with their instruments of music, and the procession moves off. At night the bride arrives, and has to wait in her chair outside while her husband dines with his friends. She has to wait a long time, and then, in the midst of a fearful volley of crackers, she goes into the house, and the first thing she does is hand food to her husband and his parents as a token of subjection.

Utilitarian Transportation

From Egypt, Burma and British Malaysia *by William Eleroy Curtis, 1905*
Carriages are useless and sedan chairs borne by two Chinese are kept for transportation purposes by every household that can afford them, while jinrikishas are used down on the sea level. Street car tracks have been laid and trolley poles have been erected for several miles on the streets around the bay; but, for some reason or another which I could not ascertain, they have never been used. Perhaps it is because the city authorities do not wish to deprive the hundreds of jinrikisha men of a living. Everything seems to be done with a view to securing the greatest good to the greatest number and employing the largest number of people possible. At a place where the macadam pavement was being repaired I noticed a roller that was hauled back and forth by twenty-eight women, most of them old and comparatively feeble, who were paid perhaps a penny a day; but that will buy rice enough to keep them alive.

"[T]he people of Hongkong are inwardly bound together by a steadily developing union of interests and responsibilities: the destiny of the one race to rule and the fate of the other to be ruled."
   E.J. Eitel, Europe in China, *1895*

Kowloon

Southern Kowloon, the area of the Mainland directly opposite Hong Kong, was ceded to the British in 1860 as part of the Convention of Peking that concluded the Second Opium War. Viewing it as an essential part of Britain's coastal defence, the area of Kowloon north of Boundary St. was leased along with the New Territories for 99 years in 1898. Kowloon developed during the Song Dynasty (960-1279) but there had been settlements in the area for much longer, as evidenced by a surviving Han Dynasty (206BC-220AD) tomb.

The name Kowloon, meaning 'Nine Dragons', is most likely a reference to the row of hills to the north including Lion Rock, though the number and mythological beast could both refer to the Chinese Emperor, which they traditionally represent. Kowloon was where the last boy Emperor of the Song Dynasty fled in 1279 after Hangzhou fell to the Mongols, and a boulder at Sung Wang Tai with an inscription memorializing his flight remains there today.

Though it saw little growth in the early years of possession, some businessmen like Paul Chater saw its great potential and invested heavily in its development. Within a short time, Kowloon had become a suburb of considerable size and an inseparable part of the Colony.

Godowns (warehouses) in Kowloon.

44

The Kowloon station of the Kowloon-Canton Railway, around the time of its opening in 1911.

A Great Extension

From Archibald R. Colquhoun's The Mastery of the Pacific, *1902*
The territory acquired at Kaulung on the neighboring mainland provides ample room for a great extension of Hong Kong, which is already being rapidly utilised. The town itself contains many handsome buildings, and the Chinese shops are famous for their store of silver, black wood furniture, and curios. A beautiful sight is the flower-market held in a side street which rises in steps, so that the masses of blooms seem to be piled one on top of the other…The extension on the mainland, however, besides serving other ends, has provided an outlet for the energies of the British, who can go over to stretch their legs, shoot, or play golf.

Gov. Matthew Nathan was responsible for significant developments in Kowloon, and the main thoroughfare of downtown Kowloon bears his name.

45

Hong Kong on Ice

From an article in Nature *by Charles Ford, describing a rare frost on Jan. 15-18, 1893*

SIR,– The unprecedented cold weather which the region about Hongkong was recently subjected to calls for some notice by this department…the temperature must have fallen on the summit to about 25° or 24° F…All vegetation throughout the hill region of the Colony was thus covered in ice, as were most other objects. Telegraph and telephone wires from Victoria Gap upwards were covered with ice 5/8 of an inch in thickness, and, in addition, carried icicles as much as three inches in length as close as they could be packed side by side. This caused many of the telephone wires to break, and the iron post at Victoria Gap which supported them was snapped off a few inches above the ground.

'Street Scene' by George Chinnery, an artist who lived in Macau and Hong Kong in the 1830s-40s

Dirty Work

Report from P.A. Surg. John McMullen, Surgeon General, on December 27, 1902
A large number of rats are killed each week under the direction of local health authorities, and, according to the medical officer of health, about 7 per cent of these are plague infected. All rats brought to the authorities are carefully examined by the city bacteriologist.

The medical officer of health informs me that formerly these rats were caught and brought in by anyone, but this has been discontinued, for the reason that about 75 per cent of the Chinese engaged in this work died of plague.

> "The Chinese rat catchers are said to be dishonest; they fail properly to label the rats, so that infected houses escape detection, and they import rats from the outside of Hongkong and label them at random. In general they are very unreliable in their work and are actuated solely by the desire to secure from anywhere the largest number of rats in order to obtain the premium offered for each."
> *Dr. Maximilian Herzog, a doctor stationed in Southeast Asia, 1904*

Kite Fighters

Mrs. Arnold Foster's In the Valley of the Yangtze, *1899*
Some Chinese kites are very cleverly made in imitation of birds, butterflies, and other things. In Hong-Kong the string attached to the kite is some-times covered with fine bits of glass, so that it cuts like a knife. The game is to get your kite up high in the air, and then see how many other kites you can cut down by cutting their strings with your own. But kites are often flown with common string, just as you fly them in England, only in China you frequently see grown-up men flying kites for their own amusement[.]

Captain Charles Elliot

Captain Charles Elliot was Hong Kong's first British administrator, serving from January to August 1841. He was sympathetic to Chinese interests and opposed to the opium trade, a man of integrity with good intentions and restrained judgment. In other words, the worst choice for the task he was handed.

Elliot became the Chief Superintendent of Trade in China upon the failure and consequent death of his overzealous predecessor, William Napier, to secure trade rights with gunboats. Commissioner Lin arrived in Canton in 1839, and seized and destroyed British opium stores. Elliot successfully negotiated the release of the captured British smugglers to Macau and later Hong Kong, but all for naught when months later a rowdy drunken group of English and American sailors clashed with Chinese locals in Kowloon, killing one. Unwilling or unable to turn them over to the Chinese authorities, the situation quickly escalated into a full-scale military conflict, the First Opium War.

With vastly superior naval power, the British easily gained the upper hand in the conflict and in January 1841, Elliot arranged to negotiate the terms of surrender with the Mandarin High Commissioner Kishen at Chuenpi. Elliot proposed the cessation of Hong Kong, free trade at Canton but suggested that Chinese would still be able to levy customs duties. Unwisely, Elliot accidentally announced the terms prior to the meeting. The terms were rejected by China and enraged British Foreign Secretary Palmerston, who immediately ordered his recall.

As a parting gift for Elliot, two typhoons hit Hong Kong in June and destroyed almost every building on the island. The good captain, still unaware that his replacement was *en route*, was shipwrecked on a tiny island by one of the storms, rescued by a Cantonese fisherman and transported to Macau shirtless with only a Manila hat, striped pants and a jacket.

Pending Her Majesty's Pleasure

Captain Charles Elliot's proclamation for the foundation of the Hong Kong colony, written aboard the HMS Wellesley on Jan. 29, 1841, just a few months before his sacking.

The island of Hongkong having been ceded to the British crown under the seal of the Imperial minister and high commissioner Keshan, it has become necessary to provide for the government thereof, pending her Majesty's further pleasure ... And I do hereby declare and proclaim that, pending Her Majesty's further pleasure, the government of the said island shall devolve upon, and be exercised by, the person filling the office of Chief Superintendent of the trade of British subjects in China for the time being…And I do further declare and proclaim, that, pending Her Majesty's further pleasure, all British subjects and foreigners residing in, or resorting to the island of Hongkong, shall enjoy full security and protection, according to the principles and practice of British law, so long as they shall continue to conform to the authority of Her Majesty's government in and over the island of Hongkong, hereby duly constituted and proclaimed…

GOD SAVE THE QUEEN

"All we wanted might have been got if it had not been for the unaccountably strange conduct of Chas. Elliot…He tried to obtain the lowest terms from the Chinese."

Queen Victoria, 1840s

"You have disobeyed and neglected your Instructions; you have deliberately abstained from employing the Force placed at your disposal; and you have without sufficient necessity accepted Terms which fall far short of those you were instructed to obtain…You have obtained the cession of Hong Kong, a bare Island with hardly a House upon it. Now it seems obvious that Hong Kong will not be a Mart of Trade, any more than Macao is so."

Foreign Secretary Palmerston to Elliot, 1841

The Scottish

As elsewhere in the Far East, the Scottish left their indelible stamp on Hong Kong. The Opium Wars were started, after all, largely at the prompting of Jardine and Matheson, both Scottish. Indeed at every step of the Colony's expansion, they were there. The Scottish Gen. J.H. Grant fought in both Opium Wars and negotiated the 1860 Convention of Peking, which resulted in the acquisition of Kowloon. James Lockhart helped define the boundaries of, and raise the first Union Jack over, the New Territories. For many years they also shaped the opinions of the Colony, as the editors of *The China Mail* and *Hongkong Telegraph* were often Scottish. Today their mark can still be felt, as many of the most successful and longest-enduring companies such as the Hongkong & Shanghai Banking Corporation and Watsons drug store were originally established by Scotsmen.

Victoria Gaol, opened in 1841, was one of the first major structures built in Hong Kong and remained in use until 2006.

Canny Scots

From Charles Wentworth Dilke's Greater Britain, *1890*
Whether it be that the Scotch emigrants are for the most part men of better education than those of other nations, of whose citizens only the poorest and most ignorant are known to emigrate, or whether the Scotchman owes his uniform success in every climate to his perseverance or his shrewdness, the fact remains, that wherever abroad you come across a Scotchman, you invariably find him prosperous and respected. The Scotch emigrant is a man who leaves Scotland because he wishes to rise faster and higher than he can at home, whereas the emigrant Irishman quits Galway or County Cork only because there is no longer food or shelter for him there. The Scotchman crosses the seas in calculating contentment; the Irishman in sorrow and despair.

The Roads of Hong Kong

From The Treaty Ports of China and Japan *by Wm. Fred. Mayers, N.B. Dennys and Chas. King, 1867*

The Roads of Hongkong are, as a rule, well made, and those constructed at a comparatively uniform level running from East to West afford some picturesque walks. Those most frequented are: the Queen's road, which extends from Tai-ping-shan, or the Chinese quarter at the West end of the island, to the other, or Eastern end, of the town; Hollywood road and its continuations on a somewhat higher level than the former; Caine Road (which extends with its continuations, from Government House to Pokfulum and is *the* Road of the island) on a higher level still; and Robinson Road, the highest in Victoria. Up to the close of 1865 there was some little danger in traversing the two latter at night if alone and unarmed, while the Western end of Victoria has ever been unsafe from the numerous Chinese bad characters who infest it...The general appearance of the more important Roads will produce a favourable effect on the minds of the visitor.

Stanley Prison

Ten days after the fall of Hong Kong to the Japanese (Christmas 1941), Allied nationals were rounded up and taken to a prison camp in Stanley on the south side of the island. About 2,800 prisoners were held at the camp, who despite crowded conditions and food shortages tried to create a sense of normalcy, organizing administrative committees, a school and even using the stage at St. Stephan's college (part of the camp) for performances. Some prisoners escaped, others were killed in the attempt, and some were granted release. More than a dozen died during an accidental American bombing, but most survived, in large part due to the help of their Chinese and non-Allied foreign friends still living in the colony. The situation is described below in an excerpt from "Behind Japanese Barbed Wire" by Geoffrey Charles Emerson, from Journal of the Hong Kong Branch of the Royal Asiatic Society, 1977. *Emerson also published* Hong Kong Internment 1942-1945 - Life in the Japanese Civilian Camp at Stanley *in 2008.*

The biggest problem throughout internment concerned food. There simply was never enough, and what there was, was very poor. The rice frequently contained dust, mud, rat and cockroach excreta, cigarette ends and even, on occasion, dead rats…The meals usually consisted of rice and a stew poured on top, made from whatever meat (usually water-buffalo meat), fish and/or vegetables were provided… The Black Market was an outstanding feature of Stanley Camp — outstanding because of its magnitude. Food, the main item of trade, of course, was brought into Camp by the guards for sale to the internees, and valuables of the internees were sent out for sale in the city. Most transactions were made via internee-traders who acted as go-betweens. One unusual feature of the Black Market in Stanley Camp was that internees could "buy" yen by writing sterling cheques to fellow internees who had extra yen. These cheques were payable after the war and were called 'duress cheques' as they had been written under duress. After the war the Hong Kong Government announced that people should not feel obligated to honour them. However, as those who signed the cheques had done so willingly and felt that in many cases they had saved them from starvation, almost all the cheques were honoured. As a result, a few of the internee-traders who held many of these cheques became wealthy.

One man was said to have done this:

1st — he traded 8 lbs. of rice for a tin of golden syrup
2nd — he sold the syrup for HK$500
3rd —he sold the HK$500 for ¥3000
4th —he sold the ¥3000 at ¥10 to £1 for a £300 cheque.

Thus his original 8 lbs. of rice, which before the war was worth about 1 shilling and 4 pence, was eventually turned into 300 pounds sterling!

Farewell to Stanley

By C.J. Norman, former internee
A Farewell to Stanley! It's over.
Of Internees there isn't a sign.
They've left for Newhaven & Dover
For Hull & Newcastle-on-Tyne.

No tales where the rumours once started.
The kitchen's devoid of its queues.
The strategists all have departed
With the lies which they peddled as 'news'.

No more of the lectures on Drama
On Beavers & Badgers & Boats,
On 'Backwards through Kent on a Llama',
And 'How to raise pedigree goats'.

No more do we carry sea water
And rations are things of the past.
Farewell to the Indian Quarter
For internment is over at last.

"The greatest difficulty we had to face in planning an escape from this camp lay in the fact that the only way out was through China. We knew neither the land nor its people, but we had heard that bandits infested the surrounding countryside. In addition, the Japs had spies in our camp."
E.D. Crossley, 1945

Prisoners from Stanley prison after Hong Kong's liberation in 1945.

Romance at Sea

A.F. Lindley (Lin-Le), British Naval officer turned Taiping rebel, in Ti-ping Tien-kwoh, *1866*

She was the daughter of a rich Macanese, who was principal owner of one of the Whampoa docks, and was also Portuguese consul at that port. Her mother was dead, and her father had determined to compel her to marry a wealthy Chilianian half-caste; in fact, everything was arranged for the marriage to take place in ten days' time. She hated the fellow, in spite of his dollars, which, it appeared, was her father's idol, and was resolved to suffer anything rather than submit. She came off to my ship to try and obtain a passage down to Hong-Kong, where she had friends who would take care of her… True to her promise, she saw me the following evening; then the next; and so for several consecutive days. It happened that, fortunately for the fulfilment of our appointments,

Marie's father never returned from the docks, at the opposite side of the river, till late in the evening. We were thus constantly thrown together, and who can wonder that we insensibly allowed ourselves to become deeply attached?

Upon the ninth day after our first meeting, my ship was undocked, and prepared to sail for Hong-Kong in the morning; the morning, too, that, as Marie told me with tears in her eyes, would usher in her bridal day. Although Marie and I had never till then spoken of love, we both knew that it was mutual, and at this moment of peril and uncertainty we threw off all disguise and expressed our true feelings for each other.

When we reach Hong-Kong, Marie landed and went to reside with her friends. She had become my betrothed, and seemed truly happy in the thought that nothing now could cause our separation.

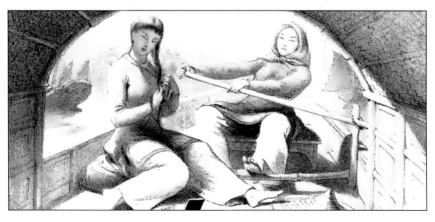

The Taipans' Club

From Twentieth Century Impressions of Hongkong, Shanghai, and other Treaty Ports of China *edited by Arnold Wright, 1908*

The Hongkong Club, or "the Club," as it is more often termed, is the premier institution of the kind in the Colony…it was inaugurated as a "Taipans' Club," for the convenience of, and as a place of meeting for, the heads of the large hongs then existing in the Colony…There are nine billiard tables, a fine bowling alley, spacious dining, reading, and general rooms, bars, and living accommodation for 34 guests…His Excellency the Governor, His Excellency the Admiral, and His Excellency the General Officer commanding the Forces are honorary members. Ordinary members are admitted only by ballot, and visitors for a term not exceeding three months may be proposed by members of the Club…The staff consists of the secretary, the assistant secretary, two European stewards, and about two hundred Chinese servants.

The second and best-known incarnation of the Hong Kong Club, built in 1897.

Through the Eye of the Needle

From The Chinese *by John Stuart Thomson, 1909*

The luxurious and hospitable Hong-Kong club, where I had the pleasure of staying for a year and a half, would be hard to surpass on Fifth Avenue or Pall Mall for accommodations and appearance. It is situated on the Praya Grand Central, in the heart of Victoria City and at the bay's edge. The Emperor of China could not be made a member on account of his color, but I have heard of one Parsee getting in through the eye of the needle, and it was said the needle was threaded by the English king. There will, however, never be another such contretemps.

Oil painting of Hong Kong in the 1860s by a Chinese artist.

Heaven or Earth?

William Martin in Understand the Chinese, *1934*

If you reach Hongkong after dark you will rub your eyes – where does the sky come to an end? Those scintillating lights, are they of earth or heaven? Are those streams of stars, prolonging the Milky Way, really a city? They must be, for at eleven o'clock they all go out. Morals are morals in the British colonies.

In the daytime the effect is no less impressive. Behind a quay of European type there is the busy life of the indigenous towns: streets mounting by stairs, sedan chairs, banners floating in the wind – authentic China. But a China of macadam roads, all climbing toward the Peak, whence you may look out over one of the finest landscapes in the world. The Europeans would not say "See Naples and die" if they had seen Kowloon Bay with its encircling mountains. And it is impossible to feel much pity for the Chinese émigrés who nurse their grievances here, in their luxurious villas, as they watch the sun go down in its glory.

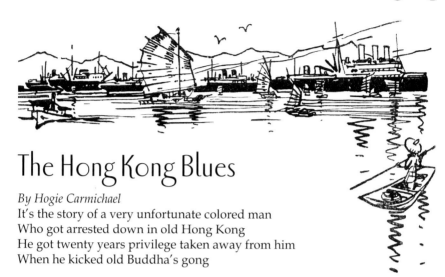

The Hong Kong Blues

By Hogie Carmichael
It's the story of a very unfortunate colored man
Who got arrested down in old Hong Kong
He got twenty years privilege taken away from him
When he kicked old Buddha's gong

And now he's poppin' the piano just to raise the price
Of a ticket to the land of the free
Well, he says his homes in Frisco where they send the rice
But it's really in Tennessee

That's why he said, "I need someone to love me
I need somebody to carry me home to San Francisco
And bury my body there
I need someone to lend me a fifty dollar bill and then
I'll leave Hong Kong behind me for happiness once again"

Won't somebody believe
I've a yen to see the Bay again
Every time I try to leave
Sweet opium won't let me fly away

I need someone to love me
I need somebody to carry me home to San Francisco
And bury my body there

That's the story of a very unfortunate colored man
Who got arrested down in old Hong Kong
He got twenty years privilege taken away from him
When he kicked old Buddha's gong

The Peak tram around the turn of the twentieth century.

Madame Randall's Honey

From The Taipans, Hong Kong's Merchant Princes *by Colin N. Criswell*

A glance at the police court records [in the colony's early years] is sufficient to show that there were numerous European prostitutes in Hong Kong, who generally took up residence in the vicinity of Hollywood Road and Lyndhurst Terrace. One aspect of local regulations is indicated by a report in which the mistress of a 'foreign brothel' was fined $100 for admitting a Chinese…For a better class of client. Madame Randall, an actress from Australia, probably has the distinction of setting up the first of these. Her renowned establishment in Lyndhurst Terrace had all the comforts of a middle-class Victorian home. Initially she solved the problem of making the gentlemen of the colony aware of her services by inserting the following advertisement:

HONEY

At Mrs Randall's — a small quantity of good Honey in small jars; also Gin, Brandy, Sherry, Port, Champagne, Claret, Bottled Beer, Porter etc etc

Lyndhurst Terrace,

Victoria, 12th June 1851.

> "A long residence in the East does not certainly improve a man's chance in the matrimonial line."
>
> *Joseph Jardine, c1850s*

The Pecking Order

A letter by Charles Richard Thomas, 14 August 1937

Every European here is waited upon hand and foot. I am myself I admit. It goes to the heads of the people who in England are nobodies. Dockyard people, petty government officials, and the like, who have created a caste which is nauseous to say the least. Naturally this caste is not recognised by the higher caste of officers and their wives and higher Government officials, nor do either caste recognise yet another group of Army family society. The sailor stands aloof – a society of his own.

Cantonese Fish Frighteners

An early description of Hong Kong fishermen in Sketches of China *by future Governor John Francis Davis, 1841*

The sight of Europeans was to these people, mostly fisherman, a novel one, for until then the spot had been seldom visited, and to such of the embassy as were accustomed to the impertinence of the Canton people, their behavior appeared very quiet and civil. We had occasion, during our stay at anchorage, to remark their singular mode of fishing. They create a horrible din by their gongs and shouting, and beat in the most frantic manner the surface of the calm water with oars and large sticks. By this process they appear to bewilder and stun the fish, and to drive them into their nets in considerable numbers. We observed, at least, that great success attended their labours. Indeed, any person, who has verified by experiment the extraordinary power of conveying sound exhibited by water, need not be surprised at the efficacy of this plan of frightening out of their wits the finny tribes, who would seem to possess the faculty of hearing in a very sensible degree.

Yeung Hau Temple in Tai O, western Lantau Island, late 19th century.

Man Overboard!

From A Merry Banker in the Far East *by Walter H. Young, 1916*
When we reached a certain quiet bay we knew of, some twenty miles from Hong Kong, we would anchor our launch; put on our bathing suits; drop into the dinghy, have a swim round and some cherry-brandy; and then go a-fishing with our little bits of dynamite tied to sticks of firewood, with a foot or two of fuse attached. Having lighted the fuse, we would chuck it far away from the boat; then lie on our oars holding ready little rope nets, tacked to the end of long bamboos. When the explosion occurred, lots of fish came stunned to the surface, and these we used to rake in for chow-chow.

On one occasion, our dinghy kept drifting nearer and nearer the dynamite, which smouldered but wouldn't go off. When we were nearly on top of it expecting at any moment to be frightfully shocked (we were too paralysed to pull away) one of our pals in the boat – a nervy chap – dived overboard in a mortal funk. Then the long-waited-for explosion exploded, and, as usual, the shock struck downwards; so our dear old pal with the other silly fishes came floating to the surface tummy topside! We didn't cook or fillet him – just smacked him to life – then passed the cherry-brandy round!

"It is with unfeigned regret and reluctance that the author states that scenes frequently occur in the public streets, and in the interior of houses, which are calculated to place the countrymen of Missionaries in an unfavourable aspect before the native mind."
Rev. George Smith, Consular Cities of China, *1847*

**B
O
O
R
D
S**

**O
L
D
T
O
M
GIN**

Sole Agents

Tel. C. 75.

CALDBECK MACGREGOR & CO., LTD.

Sir Catchick Paul Chater

Sir Catchick Paul Chater (1846-1926), a Calcutta-born Armenian, arrived in Hong Kong in 1864 as a humble bank clerk but rose to become one of the most influential businessmen in Hong Kong's history. His portfolio was diverse, ranging from real estate, warehousing and electricity to ferries, trams and even rope making. His connections were equally impressive including notables like Keswick, Kadoorie, Sassoon, Ho Tung and Mody, a veritable 19th century *Who's Who*. More than almost anyone else, he helped to reshape the physical landscape of the city, investing heavily in Kowloon before others realized its potential and spearheaded the Praya Reclamation project.

An avid horseracing enthusiast, Sir Paul (as he was known to his friends) supposedly never missed a race in sixty years. He was an active freemason and a collector of fine porcelain. He was also a pillar of his adopted British community. He served in the Legislative Council for almost twenty years and was one of the first members of the Executive Council. He gave generously to local schools and churches, and willed his palatial mansion, Marble House, to the people of Hong Kong. When he passed away, his estate was valued at $4,900,000 and, when news of his death became known, the Hong Kong Stock Exchange suspended trading for the remainder of the day.

Dining at Marble Hall

A 1923 excerpt from the diary of Commander C.H. Drage

Dec. 1st. - Woke up feeling rather the worse for wear and with a busy day ahead of me. With H.E. to lunch with Sir Paul Chater, a coloured magnate and the multi-millionaire of Hong Kong. He has a lovely house full of wonderful china, and gave us an excellent meal with superlative wine... His collection of china is well-known and, though much of it is said to be faked, the pieces are really beautiful, but the furnishing of the rest of the house is in atrocious taste...Then on to the races, which were much as on other days. After dinner to a jolly little dance in the Carlisle.

Revelation

From Henry Norman's Peoples and Politics of the Far East, *1895*

The face of Hongkong is not its fortune, and anyone merely steaming by would never guess the marvel it grows on closer acquaintance. For a few weeks' investigation transfigures this precipitous island into one of the most astonishing spots on the earth's surface. By an inevitable alchemy, the philosopher's stone of a few correlated facts transforms one's disappointment into stupefaction. Shanghai is a surprise, but Hongkong is a revelation.

The old clock tower, at the intersection of Pedder Street and Queen's road was demolished in 1908. One of its clock faces was preserved and used in the clock tower at the Kowloon-Canton Railway Station.

The Mystic City

In Shamus A'Rabbitt's
China Coast Ballads, *1938*

Here all the stars of heaven
Are nestled on the waters
Beneath the sparkling canopy of night
A thousand brilliant avenues
Come flickering as a welcome
It is the mystic city that we sight.

As mistress of old Neptune,
She sits upon the ocean–
The goddess of the world her sages plan
Her head within the heavens
Her feet to stem the tide
She watches o'er the destiny of man.

Her bosom it has nurtured
From birth to hardy childhood
An Eastern and a Western race's song
She's wed their art and science
Cementing an alliance
A glory to the ages – stands Hongkong.

Plague

After spreading rapidly across southern China, the bubonic plague struck Hong Kong via Canton in May 1894. The area around the base of Victoria Peak was the first to be affected and within weeks, thousands of mostly Chinese victims were infected.

The British authorities were initially hesitant to intervene, because many Chinese residents doubted the effectiveness of Western medicine, and it quickly became apparent that many Chinese would not report sickness to doctors. Some even took measures to hide infection for fear of having their property destroyed. The British garrison was called in to perform a door-to-door search, but this led to further anti-foreign sentiment amid rumours that the soldiers' true motive was their unsavoury yearning for Chinese women and children. Rioting began, doctors were forced to arm themselves and order was only restored with the aid of a gunboat.

The plague claimed almost 2,500 lives in '94, but re-appeared in Hong Kong regularly for the next thirty years. Various measures were proposed for controlling its spread, but with little effect and the plague became a symbol of colonial mismanagement. In 1907, for example, there was a great scandal when it was discovered that the government's sanitary specialists responsible for condemning buildings were in cahoots with property developers. The last outbreak of the plague was in 1924.

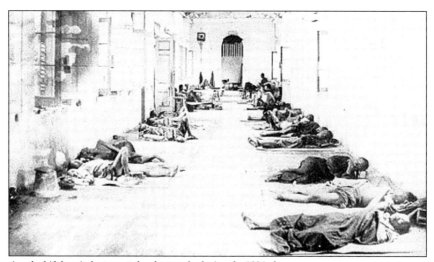

A makeshift hospital set up at the glass works during the 1894 plague.

Happy Valley Cemetery around 1910.

Swallowed Up

In John D. Ford's An American Cruiser in the East, *1898*
How full these cemeteries are! It is only about fifty years since the white man unfurled his banner and took possession of the island, but in that time the "Happy Valley" has swallowed up her victims by hundreds and by thousands. The ride back to the city is delightful, but one becomes a little serious while pondering over the causes that have filled these cemeteries in so short a time.

Beating Back the Dire Pestilence

Charles Holcombe of the Imperial Maritime Customs, 1894
Those who were able to fled from the colony, before it was too late and those who could not, went to their homes...Two of my own servants went home and died: and several rats came out in my rooms all of which died from the plague – I buried them at once and took every precaution...my wife and I fully expected every moment to be stricken with it...Many Chinese hid the bodies of their deceased relatives away in the houses so as to avoid the premises being cleaned and disinfected and the accumulated filth of years cleared away. In consequence search parties had to be organized to enter every house, and hundreds of corpses were found secreted in this manner and were buried...As all the hospitals soon became overcrowded with plague patients, mat-sheds had to be erected for their reception and treatment. At last, however, after thousands had been swept away, the colony began to shake itself free.

An American Pirate in Hong Kong

American Eli Boggs was the most notorious pirate on the South China Sea in the 1850s. A commander of as many as 40 Chinese pirate junks, Boggs earned a reputation for brutality, kidnapping and intimidation. Once he captured a group of merchants and, when they balked at his ransom, had one of them quartered and returned home in buckets. In 1857, Boggs' fleet was tracked down near Shanghai by the *H.M.S. Bittern* and he was taken captive. When tried for piracy and murder in Hong Kong, Boggs created a sensation.

A Face of Feminine Beauty

From The Times, *September 1, 1857*

His name would do for a villain of the Blackbeard class, but in form and feature he was like the hero of a sentimental novel; as he stood in the dock, bravely battling for his life, it seemed impossible that that handsome boy could be the pirate whose name had been for three years connected with the boldest and bloodiest acts of piracy. It was a face of feminine beauty. Not a down upon the upper lip; large lustrous eyes; a mouth the smile of which might woo coy maidens; affluent black hair, not carelessly parted; hands so small and so delicately white that they would create a sensation in Belgravia: such was the Hongkong pirate, Eli Boggs. He spoke for two hours in his defence, and he spoke well – without a tremor, without an appeal for mercy…The defence was, of course, false. It had been proved that he had boarded a junk, and destroyed by cannon, pistol and sword, fifteen men; and that, having forced all the rest overboard, he had fired at one of the victims, who had clutched a rope and held on astern. No witness, however, could prove that he saw a man die from a blow or a shot struck or fired by the pirate. The jury, moved by his youth and courage, and straining hard their consciences acquitted him of the murder but found him guilty of piracy.

The Taipans

In a city built for trading, the heads of the powerful firms, the 'Taipans', lived like kings. Perched on high in their mansions atop Victoria Peak, they looked down on the colony and its inhabitants like Olympian gods. They were surrounded by an army of servants who tended to their every whim, epitomizing the height of colonialism's arrogance, but also its power. No one – not even the colonial government – could challenge their effective authority.

The Taipans were hardly a homogenous group. Many were English, but a great many came from Scotland. Parsees, Jews, Indians, Armenians and Eurasians also rose to Taipan-dom. At the far reaches of the Empire, these outlying groups could thrive and attain a certain degree of social status through that great equalizer, wealth.

Governors came and went, but the Taipans and their empire remained. These were the men who created the social fabric of the colony. They established its lasting social institutions, sporting grounds, schools and churches. They laid the groundwork for the local infrastructure and expanded the waterfront. The British Empire is no more, but the Taipan's legacy endures in the names of buildings, streets and their surviving firms.

Dent's Fountain and Beaconsfield Arcade, 1860s.

> "The opening of the country is their cry, "progress" is their motto, war is their object."
> The Times, *1870*

Heavenly Splendour

From Rudyard Kipling's From Sea to Sea (Vol. 1), *1899*

The Taipan's palace, full of all things beautiful, and flowers more lovely than the gem-like cabinets they adorned, would have made happy half a hundred young men craving for luxury, and might have made them writers, singers, and poets. It was inhabited by men with big heads and straight eyes, who sat among the splendours and talked business...If I were not going to be a Burman when I die I would be a Taipan at Hong-Kong. He knows so much and he deals so largely with Princes and Powers, and he has a flag of his very own which he pins on to all his steamers.

Gone Far Indeed

From W. Somerset Maugham's "The Taipan" in On a Chinese Screen, *1922*

No one knew better than he that he was an important person. He was number one in not the least important branch of the most important English firm in China. He had worked his way up through solid ability and he looked back with a faint smile at the callow clerk who had come out to China thirty years before. When he remembered the modest home he had come from, a little red house in a long row of little red houses, in Barnes, a suburb which, aiming desperately at the genteel, achieves only a sordid melancholy, and compared it with the magnificent stone mansion, with its wide verandahs and spacious rooms, which was at once the office of the company and his own residence, he chuckled with satisfaction. He had come a long way since then. He thought of the high tea to which he sat down when he came home from school (he was at St. Paul's), with his father and mother and his two sisters, a slice of cold meat, a great deal of bread and butter and plenty of milk in his tea, everybody helping himself, and then he thought of the state in which now he ate his evening meal. He always dressed and whether he was alone or not he expected the three boys to wait at table. His number one boy knew exactly what he liked and he never had to bother himself with the details of housekeeping; but he always had a set dinner with soup and fish, entree, roast, sweet and savoury, so that if he wanted to ask anyone in at the last moment he could. He liked his food and he did not see why when he was alone he should have less good a dinner than when he had a guest.

He had indeed gone far. That was why he did not care to go home now, he had not been to England for ten years, and he took his leave in Japan or Vancouver where he was sure of meeting old friends from the China coast. He knew no one at home…he was very happy where he was, he could save money, which you couldn't do in Shanghai, and have a good time into the bargain. This place had another advantage over Shanghai: he was the most prominent man in the community and what he said went. Even the consul took care to keep on the right side of him…He flattered himself that he had the finest stable in the city. He pouted his broad chest like a pigeon. It was a beautiful day, and it was good to be alive.

Newspapers of Old Hong Kong

Old Hong Kong's English-speaking population may never have topped 10,000, but they never wanted for newspapers. The first major paper to emerge was the *China Mail* (established 1845 and closed in 1974). For years it had a monopoly on government bulletins, until the government grew unhappy with the paper's criticism and opened a newspaper of its own, the onerously boring *Government Gazette* (established 1853). In 1857, the first daily, the *Hongkong Daily Press*, was launched and, like the *China Mail* before it, it took a tough line on the government, occasionally landing the editors for both in Victoria Gaol. Not far behind, the evening *Hongkong Telegraph* (est. 1881), was hugely popular due to its colourful and frequently libellous early editor, Robert Fraser-Smith, who also managed to get thrown in prison, though for less virtuous reasons: he alleged a Publics Work Department foreman was a rapist. Last, but certainly not least, of the major players was the popular *South China Morning Post* (est. 1903). Starting as an eight-page daily, it more than doubled in size during its first 20 years, merged with the *Telegraph* in 1916 and remains to this day a highly respected newspaper.

Opening editorial of the South China Morning Post, *6 November 1903*

"The modern newspaper has taken the place of the old-time ambassador. The cynic has said the ambassador is sent abroad to lie for the good of his country. The newspaper is sent abroad to tell the truth for the good of humanity."

Enchanting Djunks

In Count Fritz von Hochberg's, An Eastern Voyage, *1910*

I love the Chinese. The enchanting djunks all tied to the piers for the New Year's week, when no Chinese will do any work, but everybody has to don new clothes and give themselves up to frolicking and the letting-off of as many crackers as his purse will allow him. And yet all the fascinating, though not always strictly clean nor odoriferous life that is going on in these djunks, from which I always find it so difficult to tear myself away, is the same. The cooking, washing, dressing of those fascinating Chinese doll-children, and their delightful ways and plays!

"Excitement runs high, language is free, and collisions appear imminent, but the smoothness and precision with which the junkmaster works his junk through the crowded shipping speaks a lot for his skill and the handiness of his rig."

Ivon Arthur Donnelly, Chinese Junks and Other Native Craft, *1924*

Governors of Hong Kong

Captain Charles Elliot (unofficial)	Jan. – Aug. 1841
Sir Henry Pottinger	Aug. 1841- May 1844
Sir John Francis Davis	May 1844 – Mar. 1848
Sir George Bonham	Mar. 1848 – Apr. 1854
Sir John Bowring:	Apr. 1854 – May 1859
Sir Hercules Robinson	Sept. 1859 – Mar. 1865
Sir Richard Graves MacDonnell	Mar. 1866 – Apr. 1872
Sir Arthur Edward Kennedy	Apr. 1872 – Mar. 1876
Sir John Pope Hennessey	Apr. 1877 –Mar. 1882
Sir George Ferguson Bowen	Mar. 1883 – Dec. 1885
Sir George William DesVœux	Oct. 1887 – May 1891
Sir William Robinson	Dec. 1891 – Jan. 1898
Sir Henry Arthur Blake	Nov. 1898 – Jul. 1903
Sir Matthew Nathan	Jul. 1904 – Apr. 1907
Sir Frederick Lugard	Jul. 1907 – Mar. 1912
Sir Frances Henry May	Jul. 1912 – Sept. 1918
Sir Reginald Edward Stubbs	Sept. 1919 – Oct. 1925
Sir Cecil Clementi	Nov. 1925 – Feb. 1930
Sir William Peel	May 1930 – May 1935
Sir Andrew Caldecott	Dec. 1935 – Apr. 1937
Sir Geoffrey Northcote	Nov. 1937 – Sept. 1941
Sir Mark Aitchison Young	Sept. 1941 – Dec. 1941 and
	May 1946 – May 1947
Sir Alexander Grantham	Jul. 1947 – Dec. 1957
Sir Robert Brown Black	Jan. 1958 – Mar. 1964
Sir David Clive Crosbie Trench	Apr. 1964 – Oct. 1971
Sir Murray MacLehose	Nov. 1971 – Apr. 1982
Sir Edward Youde	May 1982 – Dec. 1986
Sir David Wilson	Apr. 1987 – Jul. 1992
Christopher Francis Patten	Jul. 1992 – Jun. 1997

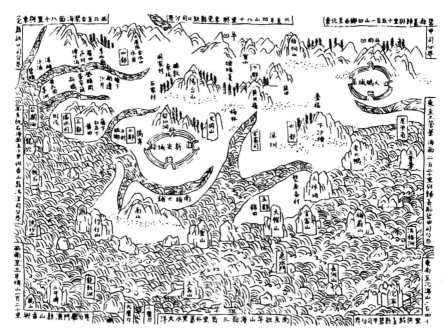

Top: A map of Xin'an County in 1819, before the large island, southeast of the Mainland was known as Hong Kong.

Bottom: A corresponding British map from 1898.

73

Temple of Vice

It is hardly surprising that a colony founded by opium merchants would boast more than a few users. Most regular users of opium were of the Chinese lower-classes, though Western sailors and even those of higher classes snuck a puff in here and there. Opium divans were outlawed in 1908, but use of the drug was not criminalized until 1946. The following fictional account of an opium den is from R.M. Ballantyne's Under the Waves, 1876.

In a certain street of Hong-Kong there stands one of those temples in which men devote themselves to the consumption of opium, that terrible drug which is said to destroy the natives of the celestial empire more fatally than "strong drink" does the peoples of the west. In various little compartments of this temple, many celestials lay in various conditions of debauch. Among them was a stout youth of twenty or so. He was in the act of lighting the little pipe from which the noxious vapour is inhaled. His fat and healthy visage proved that he had only commenced his downward career.

He had scarce drawn a single whiff, however, when a burly sailor-like man in an English garb entered the temple, went straight to the compartment where our beginner reclined, plucked the pipe from his hand, and dashed it on the ground.

"I *know'd* ye was here," said the man, sternly, "an' I *said* you was here, an' sure haven't I *found* you here—you spalpeen! You pig-faced bag o' fat! What d'ee mane by it, Chok-foo? Didn't I say I'd give you as much baccy as ye could chaw or smoke an ye'd only kape out o' this place? Come along wid ye!"

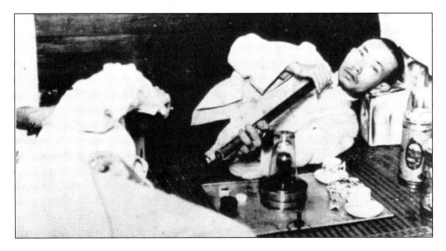

Praya Central and Ferry Station, Hongkong.

"Hongkong has now no connection whatever with China, being entirely a British possession, and has been converted from a barren rock to a most lovely, thriving and important commercial town and naval base, and is the greatest triumph of British enterprise and material civilisation that I know of."

Oliver G. Ready, Life and Sport in China, *1904*

Out of Touch

From My Life in China and America *by Yung Wing, 1909*

I was not aware that by going into the British Colony in Hong Kong to become an attorney, I was stepping on the toes of the British legal fraternity [who] banded themselves together against me, because…if I were allowed to practice my profession, they might as well pack up and go back to England…A retrospective view of my short experience in Hong Kong convinced me that it was after all the best thing that I did not succeed in becoming a lawyer in Hong Kong…I could not have come in touch with the leading minds of China, had I been bound up in that rocky and barren Colony.

The New Territories

In the late 19th century, the territorial game was heating up, with Russia, America, Germany, France and Japan pushing to destabilize British colonial supremacy in Asia. Britain partially responded by annexing 355 square-miles of sparsely populated land and over 200 islands around Hong Kong known as the 'New Territories'. It was hoped by Hong Kong Council Member Henry Black that the villagers in the area, mostly Hakka and Punti, would "accept the jurisdiction of Great Britain with equanimity and pleasure", but this was hardly the case. In 1899, early British buildings in Tai Po disrupted the local *Feng Shui* and Her Majesty's army was forced to repel armed local resistance. For many years, the only access to the Territories was by rail, and few Europeans bothered to build houses there. The New Territories were largely undeveloped and, for the most part, the British left them that way until the late 20th century, with the administration resting mainly with village elders.

The raising of the flag over Tai Po on 17 April 1899.

> "Can he so far have lost his head that he wants to annex Canton?"
> *Colonial Office comment on Governor Robinson, 1898*

Chinese Folk No Good

From Griffith Taylor's "China. Among the Hakka Tribes", 12 Feb. 1927

Let us wander through some of these villages, which are scattered through Kowloon Territory between Hongkong and Canton. In each little village are several hundred acres of vegetable gardens…[In a large dwelling] the head of the manor met us. He spoke a little English, and courteously invited us to inspect the main hall and the shrine…He was proud of his Hakka descent, and remarked "Chinese folk no good." (As the Chinese express the same opinion of the Hakka, we may take it that no man is the best judge of the comparative virtues of his own race!)

Toil, Toil on Every Side!

From E. Burton Holmes, The Burton Holmes Lectures, Vol. V, *1901*
My first sortie is to the Chinese tailor to order suits of white, which are made in no time, for practically nothing – about one dollar and seventy-five cents a suit. The cost of laundering is only five cents each. We elbow our way in Queen's Road, the principal thoroughfare, through busy crowds, along the arcaded sidewalks; we see myriads of beautiful brown legs, with splendid brown bodies above them, bodies nude to the waist, backs streaming with warm rain, wide straw hats dripping water; calm coolie faces wet with sweat. Toil, toil on every side! for all these brown men are hauling jinrikishas or carrying chairs, suspended from long bamboo poles…The morning of our arrival a jinrikisha coolie fell dead between the shafts, while running with a passenger. The dead man was picked up, placed in his own jinrikisha, and rushed away; the first ride he had ever had, and the last.

Boat People

In A Voyage in the 'Sunbeam' *by Annie Allnut Brassey, 1881*
Off the town of Victoria the crowd of shipping is immense, and it became a difficult task to thread our way between the fleets of sampans and junks. The latter are the most extraordinary-looking craft I ever saw, with high, overhanging sterns and roll, or rather draw, up sails, sometimes actually made of silk, and puffed like a lady's net ball-dress. Then their decks are so crowded with lumber, live and dead, that you wonder how the boats can be navigated at all…The sampans are long boats, pointed at both ends, and provided with a small awning. They have deep keels; and underneath the floor there is one place for a cooking fire, another for an altar, and a third where the children are stowed to be out of the way. In these sampans whole families, sometimes five generations, live and move and have their being. I never shall forget my astonishment when, going ashore very early one morning in one of these strange craft, the proprietor lifted up what I had thought was the bottom of the boat, and disclosed three or four children, packed away as tight as herrings, while under the seats were half-a-dozen people of larger growth. The young mother of the small family generally rows with the smallest baby strapped on to her back, and the next-sized one in her arms, whom she is also teaching to row. The children begin to row by themselves when they are about two years old. The boys have a gourd, intended for a life-preserver, tied round their necks as soon as they are born. The girls are left to their fate, a Chinaman thinking it rather an advantage to lose a daughter or two occasionally…Many of these sampan people have never set foot on shore in their lives, and this water-life of China is one of the most extraordinary features of the country.

Woman the Ship

"Letters from Hong Kong and Macao" in The New Monthly Magazine and Humorist, *1844*

When seated [the passenger] may amuse himself by a closer inspection than he has yet made of those fair creatures whose solicitations for his patronage nearly stunned him, and his observations will enable him to perceive that each tanka-boat is "womaned" by two women...one of the women is old, with a coloured handkerchief on her head, and tied under her chin, and that she sculls in the stern of the boat, while the other is very young, and tolerably good-looking, and with uncovered head, and her hair which is fine and beautifully black, and gathered into a large plaited tail.

Causeway Bay in the early 20th century.

"Good old place, Hong Kong! Th' finest port I ever went to, an' I've had some good times there...."

Lincoln Colcord, "Carrying Sail", 1914

As Ill as You Wish

In Seaports of the Far East, *Allister Macmillan, 1925*

In the Chinese tea houses you drink as much as you wish, and a waiter brings you cakes interminably until a big pyramid is formed. You pay for what you eat; but, for the foreign stomach, the delicacies are to be admired from afar. The Chinese has a sweet tooth, and gives zest to his confections by the judicious addition of pieces of pork fat. The foreigner can become as ill as he would wish for the expenditure of a few cents. The restaurants are better visiting. They are mostly congregated in one area, at West Point (Shek Tong Tsui), which nightly is a blaze of lights, one of the sights of the city. There the extravagant ones foregather in their long silk coats, reinforced, for ceremony, with little black satin or alpaca jackets, to eat expensive, well-prepared and totally unnecessary sharks' fins, chickens' wings stuffed, and much else — and to have singing girls screech to them and pretty painted maidens sit behind their chairs and talk to them.

"At the races in Hongkong, stalls for the sale of dogs' flesh are opened for the three or four days, confirming the foreigner in his opinion that Chinese live on dogs, but at no other time are any stalls of the kind to be found in the Colony."

J. Dyer Ball, Things Chinese, *1903*

Note on the Island of Hong-Kong

"Note on the Island of Hong-Kong" by A.R. Johnston, 1844

The island of Hong-Kong, seen from a distance at sea, is, like all the islands on this coast of China, precipitous and uninviting. Its high hills often terminate in sharp peaks, and are thickly strewed with masses of black rock, of primitive formation, frequently piled upon one another in a most remarkable and some-times fantastic manner, with here and there two or three lower hills, covered with gravel and sand. From the summit to the water's edge there are few or no trees; and…they might be supposed to be quite barren…There are no towns on the island, excepting the flourishing one of Victoria, which was founded by the English in 1841, and formally ceded to the British crown under the Nankin treaty. This town is fast springing into importance, and a 50-foot road runs through it for more than 3 miles…The village of Chek-choo is the largest and most important one on the island, and a large detachment of European troops are stationed there. The population of this village amounts to 800…The people are employed in trading, in farming, and in curing, fish…No public buildings were found on any part of the island of Hong-Kong when it was first occupied by the English, except a small tumble-down Chinese house at Chek-choo, and another at Shek-pie-wan, where the petty mandarins stopped occasionally, and three Chinese temples, one at Chek-choo, one near Soo-kun-poo and the third and finest at Shek-pie-wan…The existence of this last temple, with the ru-ins of many houses in the same vicinity, gives rise to the impression that Shek-pie-wan has seen better days; and it is known to have been one of the principal resorts of the pirates when they infested this coast of China many years ago; and that it would again lately have been so had the island of Hong-Kong, not been occupied by the English, is more than probable…The only animals found on the island are a few small deer, a sort of armadillo, and a land-tortoise. There are several sorts of snakes, but no one has yet been found to suffer from their bite.

Aberdeen, in south Hong Kong, was the first site on the island visited by the British in 1818.

Melting Away in Hong Kong

The heat of Hong Kong was a matter of grave concern. In 1850, more than a third of the 59th British Regiment, charged with developing the island, perished due to the heat and corresponding tropical illnesses. 'Death vacancies' became a half-serious joke among the soldiers, who eventually helped to clear the island of much of its malaria. Still, aside from the lucky few rich enough to afford breezy retreats on the Peak, the summer months required a high tolerance for discomfort.

Summer in the City

From The Peoples and Politics of the Far East *by Henry Norman, 1895*
One of the chief summer problems of Hongkong is determining whether the mushrooms which grow on your boots during the night are edible or not. The damp is indescribable. Moisture pours down the walls; anything left alone for a couple of days – clothes, boots, hats, portmanteaus – is covered with mold. Twenty steps in the open air and you are covered in perspiration. Then there are the cockroaches, to say nothing of the centipede whose bite may lay you up for a month.

"If you live on the Peak your clothes rot; if you live below, you rot."
Rev. E.J. Hardy, 1905

Chinese laundry, drying in the sun.

> "Hong Kong is alternately described as unquestionably healthy and deplorably sickly; as pleasantly cool and intolerably hot; as replete with interest and a desert of dullness; as hospitably sociable and savagely churlish – by the large majority, perhaps, as a place of exile, and by the minority as a fascinating residence."
>
> *From* English Life in China *by Major Henry Knollys,* 1885

John Chinaman at Home

In Due West *by Maturin Murray Ballou, 1884*

Imagine a short, slouchy figure, with sloping eyes, a yellow complexion, features characterized by a sort of low cunning, a shaved head with a pigtail, clad in a loose cloth blouse, half shirt and half jacket, continuations not exactly pants nor yet a petticoat, and shoes thick-soled and shearing upwards like a Madras surf-boat, and you have John Chinaman as he appears at home… John eats principally rice. It is in fact the basis of all his dishes, which are varied by the addition of dried fish and vegetables, adding occasionally such portions of animals as are usually thrown away by civilized people. Rats, cats, and dogs are not declined by his omnivorous appetite, and he is charged with craving nearly all sorts of vermin, such as snakes, slugs, scorpion's eggs, and caterpillars, which he complacently adds to his stews.

Blind Minstrels

Thomas Lyster in Kowloon June 27, 1865, from With Gordon in China, *1891*
The Chinese sing most wonderful songs, and play some really pretty tunes on an instrument like a guitar. I wish I was musical enough to keep them in my head and write them for you. I am sure you would imitate them capitally. Their minstrels are generally blind. Opposite to where I lived in Hong-Kong a woman used to sing for hours at a time in a loud, melancholy voice: all her tunes ended in a plaintive quavering a, aa.

Salisbury Road, 1910.

A Mere Spectator

In Richard Mason's, *The World of Suzie Wong, 1957*
At first Hong Kong with its teeming, jostling populace, its atmosphere tingling with activity and excitement had been too stimulating, too confusing; the impression had whirled in my head too swiftly to record. "I must let it take shape," I had thought. "It'll be all right in a week or two." I had been able to find no centre of interest, no point of beginning... Then I had begun to understand. My work had always depended on a sympathetic feeling, on a sense of identity with the people I sketched or drew; and here I was a mere spectator in the streets, making my occasional sorties from another world. A great wall divided me from the Chinese—and how could it be otherwise, living in Sunset Lodge.

84

I Could Just Spit

In Rudyard Kipling's From Sea to Sea *(Vol. 1), 1899*
I was proud when I saw the shipping at Singapur, but I swell with patriotism as I watch the fleets of Hong-Kong from the balcony of the Victoria Hotel. I can almost spit into the water; but many mariners stand below and they are a strong breed.

Hong-Kong Foot

"Politics Determine Chinese Health" from The Science News-Letter, *1929*
A fungus infection of the foot, known as Hong-kong foot, is very common. It is spread by the barefoot coolies, but shod Mandarins and foreigners also acquire it.

"It may be novel to some in this country to learn that there are about 1,250,000 Celestials living under our flag."
J.A. Baines', "The Population of the British Empire", 1906

Rumblings of War

Carveth Wells' North of Singapore *(1940), describing Hong Kong in 1939*
Hongkong was teeming with excitement on Sunday evening, September 3rd. War had been talked about, of course, but when newsboys began racing through the streets at seven o'clock, with the official news that it had been declared, it came as a shock, especially to those who, like myself, had experienced the last World War. Almost instantly the streets were thronged with excited people, telling one another the dreadful news as if it were something to be glad about. I could not understand this until I began talking to some Englishmen in the lobby of the Hongkong Hotel. One of them said: "I'm glad the suspense is over. Damn Hitler anyway. Now we know where we are; it's Germany or the British Empire. This time, by God, we'll finish the job we left undone in 1918. Treaty of Versailles too harsh, they told us. Not harsh enough, by a damn sight."

"What's Japan going to do?" I enquired… Remembering a conversation I had had with a Japanese in which he had told me that when the time came Japan would capture Hongkong in two days, I asked an Englishman the same question and received the reply: "One day."

No Way Out

From the diary of Barbara C. Redwood, 1941
(Dec. 8) "At 10 to 8 Bevan said war had been declared between Britain & America, & Japan, & just after 8 o'clock the air raid syrens sounded. At about 10.30 the all clear went & it was said 1 bomb had dropped in Sspo. [Sham Shui Po] causing many casualties. At 1.30 the syrens went again & there was quite a lot of A.A. fire. I thought they were all bombs at first. I saw 3 'planes high up being chased away to Lyemoon. It's hardly worth writing diary because I can't visualize us ever getting out of this, but I want to try to believe in a future."

"Black Christmas"

R.S.M. Charles Ford describing the fall of Hong Kong to the Japanese on December 25, 1941 in The Battle for Hong Kong

Xmas Day, and, I imagine, the most memorable one of all time…This is a bitter moment, for none ever expected Hong Kong to surrender, and men are crying…Many of the men are all for fighting on, but where organised resistance has failed, indiscriminate bands cannot succeed in an island so small as this.

Assorted Cruelties

From the probably apocryphal I Escaped from Hong Kong *by Jan Henrik Marsman, 1943*

I saw the Japanese wantonly torture and finally murder bound British officers and soldiers in Hong Kong. I saw them jab helpless civilian prisoners with bayonets. I saw them slowly starve British and American babies, and I still wake up in the middle of the night hearing the feeble wails of those infant victims. I saw Hirohito's savages outdo one another in practicing assorted cruelties on captured Canadians, Chinese, Indian and English soldiers.

Eurasians

Intimate relations between the Chinese and Europeans were generally frowned upon in Hong Kong. The British colonial system depended in large part on notions of racial superiority and traditional Chinese culture, which emphasizes ancestry and familial bonds, no less so. Yet despite these pressures, more and more 'Eurasians' (half-Chinese half-European) were born on the island every year.

Straddling two cultures but often accepted by neither, Eurasians' role was ill-defined and often unpleasant socially. Their knowledge of both cultures (and languages) made them valuable liaisons, and eventually earned them the trust of the British, though for the wrong reasons: they were viewed as more trustworthy than the Chinese because of their whiteness. Many worked in secondary bureaucratic posts and some even in high-ranking (though non-European) positions at major hongs. The Eurasian Ho brothers – Robert Ho Tung, Ho Kam Tung and Ho Fook – amassed considerable fortunes in business and became one of the wealthiest families in the colony.

> "Everything that brings the East and West together and helps each to understand the other better, is good. The offspring from such mixed unions inherit the good points of both sides."
> *Wu Tingfang, 1914*

D'Aguilar Street, 1925.

Hongkong's Most Tragic Product

I. Epstein's "Hongkong: Past and Present" in Far Eastern Survey, *1946*
The Eurasian is Hongkong's most tragic product. His initial physical and mental endowments combine the best of both races. But he is condemned to grow up culturally sterile and socially displaced, into a predetermined "buffer" role as non-commissioned officer (very carefully prevented from reaching commissioned rank) in the established hierarchy. He does not "belong" anywhere, generally speaks both languages, but is literate only in English. It takes a really exceptional individual to transcend this terrible combination of circumstances.

Robert Ho Tung

No one embodied the East meets West success story of Old Hong Kong more than its 'Grand Old Man', Sir Robert Ho Tung. Of humble origins, Ho Tung was born in 1862 to a European father and Cantonese mother. He received a British education, but strongly identified with Chinese culture throughout his life. In 1883, after only three years in the service of Jardine Matheson, he was promoted to comprador, the highest ranking Chinese position in the company. By 1889, he branched out on his own and eventually came to own 18 companies along the Chinese coast (with interests in several more) and tremendous real estate holdings.

Though a British citizen, Ho Tung was also a fiercely patriotic Chinese, and an important leader in both communities. Ho Tung founded the Chinese Club in response to Chinese exclusion from the Hong Kong Club, and helped build schools and hospitals. Through generous donations, he supported both Sun Yat-sen's revolution and the Allied war effort in WWI, earning him a knighthood for the latter.

Sir Robert Ho Tung (second from right) and family at Idlewild, one of their many homes.

Sir Robert had two wives, eleven children (one adopted and ten with wife Clara) and numerous residences, one of which made him the first Chinese to live on the Peak despite laws prohibiting non-Europeans. Ho Tung passed away in 1956 after almost a century as one of the colony's leading businessmen, and many of his offspring would follow in his footsteps.

The Simplest Thing in the World

Thomas Sutherland, founder of Hongkong & Shanghai Banking Corp., describing the bank's origins

I happened to be in the beginning of the year 1864, a passenger on a small P. and O. steamer…There were on board that ship a number of copies of Blackwood's magazine which contained articles on the subject of banking and I absorbed these articles: they fascinated me. I have never had a banking account in my life. I had only an account with a compradore [Chinese business manager] which was generally overdrawn; but it appeared to one that, if a suitable opportunity occurred, one of the very simplest things in the world would be to start a bank in China more or less founded upon Scottish principles.

The Premier Bank

A.M. Thomson in Twentieth Century Impressions of Hongkong, Shanghai, and other Treaty Ports of China, *1908*

Largely owing to able management and to the foresight of successive directors, the Hongkong and Shanghai Banking Corporation is to-day the premier bank of the East. Its history is one of extraordinary prosperity, and though at one time heavy losses were encountered, the tide soon became once more favourable, and upon it the Corporation has been carried to its present strong position in the financial world.

The Hongkong & Shanghai Banking Corporation established the Hong Kong Mint in 1866, creating a unified currency, the Hong Kong dollar. The above $5 and $10 notes are from the late 1930s.

"Never break your word with a Chinese, for he'll never break his with you."

Sir Thomas "Lucky" Jackson, Chief Manager of the Hongkong and Shanghai Banking Corporation 1876-1902

Honkers and Shankers: Colloquial name for the
Hong Kong & Shanghai Banking Corporation.

Wardley House, the first home to the Hongkong & Shanghai Banking Corp. from 1865-1882.

The Peak in 1908

Ascending on High

From Things Chinese *by J. Dyer Ball, 1903*

Ages ago, a Chinese received a warning that a dreadful catastrophe would happen to him and his family. To avert it he escaped to the heights; and in commemoration of this event, on the ninth day of the ninth moon, many Chinese take a holiday, or an excursion of a few hours, to some neighbouring hill, or mountain. The Peak tramway in Hongkong, providing a convenient mode of reaching a summit, is largely availed of, to the wonderment of the English traveller, who is at a loss to understand why such an exodus of natives from the town is taking place. About 3000 usually take advantage of this convenient mode of ascent...Dressed in their gala-day best, with silks and satins galore, and with happy faces, family groups may be seen wandering along the mountain roads, while troops of friends and acquaintances may be noticed chatting their loudest and enjoying the treat of a whiff of fresh air after months of confinement in narrow streets and close shops. Up at the Peak itself, the base of the flag-staff is black with human beings, who, from the distance, look like ants on a lump of sugar[.]

Sport and Leisure

J.W. Bains, Sports Editor of the China Mail, *1908*

It is questionable whether in any other part of His Majesty's dominions sport has so many adherents proportionately as are to be found within the narrow confines of Hongkong. Even on the most sultry day in midsummer, when the extreme humidity of the atmosphere invests almost every one with a feeling of lassitude, relief is gained by "a dip in the briny"…Among the most prominent branches of sport are horse-racing, cricket, football (both Rugby and Association), golf, athletics, yachting, lawn tennis, and swimming. But, in addition, lawn and alley bowls, hockey, rifle shooting, snipe and pigeon shooting, racquets, turtle hunting, and polo receive attention during the year.

Hong Kong Clubs

Listed in the 1918 Rosenstock's Directory

Hongkong Corinthian Yacht Club
The Catholic Union (a club for young men)
Civil Service Cricket Club
Club Lusitano
Craigengower Cricket Club
Hongkong Club
Hongkong Cricket Club
Hongkong Cricket League
Hongkong Jockey Club
Hongkong Polo Club
Kowloon Bowling Green Club
Kowloon Cricket Club
Peak Club
Royal Hongkong Golf Club
Royal Hongkong Yacht Club
United Services Recreation Club

The Hong Kong cricket team in 1891, a year before most of its members were tragically lost at sea to a typhoon while returning from a match in Shanghai.

Colonial Administration

As goes the adage, "Those who cannot remember the past are condemned to repeat it". By this measure, Old Hong Kong never had a chance. Its Governors and administrators were largely ignorant of Asia and its culture, and the colony's special circumstances. By the time most of them had learned enough to correct earlier mistakes, they were shipped off to the next post to make way for more doomed administrators. The Legislative Council was similarly deficient and rampant corruption at all levels of government made things even worse. The majority of the population, the Chinese, were never represented. The government was often accused of bungling or directly causing crises, such as the plagues outbreaks that hit the colony almost every year from 1894 to the 1920s and a dire shortage of water in the early 1900s.

Hong Kong City Hall, early 1900s.

A Storm in a Teapot

From an article in The Times *that caused much outrage in Hong Kong, March 15, 1859*
Hong Kong is always connected with...some discreditable internal squabble. Every official's hand is there against his neighbour. The Governor has run away to seek health or quiet elsewhere. The newspaper proprietors were, of late, all more or less in prison or going to prison or coming out of prison, on prosecutions by some one or more of the incriminated or incriminating officials. A dictator is needed, a sensible man, a man of tact and firmness. We cannot be always investigating a storm in a teapot where each individual tea-leaf has its dignity and its grievance.

The Common Right of Englishmen

An extract from a petition to the British Government by Unofficial Legislative Council Member, T.H. Whitehead, signed by 90% of British ratepayers
Those who have the knowledge and the experience are naturally the Unofficial Members, who have been elected and appointed as possessing these very qualifications, who have passed large portions of their lives in the Colony, and who either have permanent personal interests in it, or bold prominent positions of trust which connect them most closely with its affairs…On the other hand the offices occupied by the Official Members are only stepping stones in an official career…Your petitioners fully recognise that in a Colony so peculiarly situated on the borders of a great Oriental Empire, and with a population largely composed of aliens whose traditional and family interests and racial sympathies largely remain in that neighboring Empire, special legislation and guardianship are required…All your petitioners claim is the common right of Englishmen to manage their local affairs, and control the expenditure of the Colony, where Imperial considerations are not involved.

"Such a Council may suit the Pacha of Egypt, but in a British Colony it is shameful."
A Hong Kong journalist, late 1800s

In the Shadow of Weakness

Alfred Cunningham, The French in Tonkin and South China, *1902*
In Hongkong we suffer continually from the shortsighted and clumsy policy of our early officials, and the Government of to-day instead of recognising this stultifies itself in endeavouring to vindicate past blunders by a patch-work policy of administration, opposes freedom of action, shirks wholesome expenditure on public works, and avoids a modern municipal system.

95

MENU.

1. Birds' Nest Soup.   2. Stewed Shell Fish.   3. Cassia Mushrooms.
4. Crab and Sharks' Fins.   5. Roast Beef (à l'Anglaise).
6. Roast Chicken and Ham.   7. Pigeons' Eggs.
8. 'Promotion' (Boiled Quail, &c.).   9. Fried Marine Delicacies.
10. Roast Turkey and Ham (à l'Anglaise).
11. Fish Gills.   12. Larded Quails.   13. Sliced Teal.
14. Peking Mushrooms.   15. Roast Pheasant (à l'Anglaise).
16. Winter Mushrooms.   17. Roast Fowl and Ham.
18. Bêche-de-Mer.   19. Sliced Pigeon.
20. Snipe (à l'Anglaise).   21. Macaroni (à la Peking).

SIDE DISHES.

Cold Roast Sucking Pig.
Cold Roast Fowl.   Cold Roast Duck.
Cold Roast Mutton.

TABLE DISHES.

Cold Sausages.
Prawns.   Preserved Eggs.   Livers.
&c.,   &c.,   &c.

FRUITS.

Preserved Apples.
Citrons.   Tientsin Pears.   Pomegranates.   Carambolas.
Greengages.   Pine Apples.
&c.,   &c.,   &c.

PASTRY.

Sweet Lotus Soup.   Almond Custard.   Rice.
&c.,   &c.,   &c.

WINES.

Champagne (Krug).
Claret.   Orange Wine.   Rice Wine.   Rose Dhu.
'Optimus' Wine.   Pear Wine.

A menu for a Cantonese dinner served to the Duke of Connaught in 1890.

A Cantonese Gastronomic Adventure

William Des Vœux, describing a dinner party he braved as governor of Hong Kong in My Colonial Service, *1903*

After I had overcome a strong disinclination to eat at all, and had managed to taste such things as bird's-nest soup and sharks' fins, a suspicious-looking species of fungus, and eggs said to be fifty years old, my very visible illness stood me in good stead as an excuse for making no further efforts…A curious and objectionable feature of the entertainment was the presence at a different table of some painted girls. These now and then came up to one or other of the guests, who was expected to drink her health and to turn up his glass to show it was emptied, the girl doing the same, and — horrible to relate — spitting afterwards. I managed to escape being called upon to undergo this ordeal, or my objection to do so might have marred what was considered a highly successful entertainment…Mr. Lockhart (the official protector of Chinese), who sat opposite to me, attacked all the dishes like a man, and would alone have redeemed the credit of our party with the Chinese for gastronomic taste. Possibly having been for some years in China, he had become accustomed to what European new-comers are apt to regard as repulsive. Otherwise his control of the facial muscles was almost superhuman. Anderson and Bethell, though I could hear them decorously protesting how each dish was even more delicious than the last, did not appear to be able to manage more than a few mouthfuls, and I could see they had hard work to prevent making wry faces. Their struggles to assume an expression of ecstatic delight were edifying. These were evidently not observed by our hosts, and their praiseworthy efforts to please were so successful that one of my neighbours remarked to me, it was a pity I was so unwell, or I should doubtless have enjoyed my dinner as much as my staff were doing…Afterwards there was a theatrical performance in an adjoining room, with the gorgeous tawdry dresses, absurd gesticulations, falsetto screaming, and unutterable dullness which are characteristic of Chinese plays. After sitting through more than an hour of it, I was glad to get into the air and into my coolie chair, more thankful than I can say that the duty was accomplished.

Jonathan Samuel Swire

The Englishman J.S. Swire, fresh from a successful stint in Australian textiles and beer, arrived on the China coast in 1866, sensing the potential of the Far East. In his first month, he bought out his business' Shanghai agent, registered a hong – Butterfield and Swire or 'Taikoo' ('Great and Ancient') – and bought a stake in a shipping fleet. He was smart and aggressive, recruiting Chinese and foreign allies, and keeping costs low. Sensing a weakness in the older hongs' monopolies, he attacked them head on and, miraculously, became wildly successful when other firms were reeling under a disastrous economy.

Swire was a single-minded and methodical businessman, who learned from mistakes (others and his own), but was difficult to work with. Upon Butterfield's departure, after less than three years with the Hong, Swire remarked, "Mr B. retired from our firm at my suggestion – he was grasping and bothered me." As an employer, he was somewhat stingy with pay (but generous with bonuses), and required abstention from drink and gambling (never mind his earlier work for Guinness).

By the time he died in 1898, he was a well-respected and admired leader. His firm was a major force on the China coast with a fleet of almost thirty ships and the world's largest sugar refinery at the time. Swire (as the company is now known) is still a significant player in Hong Kong today.

> "I was much struck with the man. I fancy he is a person who lives by and for business alone…He will be a tremendous success or as 'damnable a fizzle' as Abe Lincoln's hatchet."
> *Frank Forbes of Russell's hong*

[T]he Firm do not approve of their Employees being interested in Race Ponies and that to so interest themselves, in future, will certainly prejudice their chance of promotion.
1900 Butterfield and Swire memo

Tiger Attack!

The March 8, 1915 Hongkong Telegraph *describes a rare instance of a tiger attack in the New Territories*

In Sheung Shui, this morning, the villagers having complained to the police of the presence of a tiger in the locality, P.C.Croucher and the constable...went out to investigate the complaint...A coolie standing close by carelessly threw a stone into the bush [and] a monster tiger, likened to the size of a pony, sprang from the bush, caught P.C.Croucher in his claws, and—though the constable is some six foot in height, and turns the scale at fifteen stone—it tossed him about like a shuttlecock. His friend went to his assistance and...fired two shots...One of the shots is supposed to have struck the tiger and he dashed back into the bush, but not before he had torn four holes in the back and one in the shoulder of the constable, severely lacerating his body all down one side.

The 'Sheung Shui Tiger', killed by Donald Burlingame A.S.P. Accounts vary on the number killed by the tiger, though it was probably between one and three persons.

Criminality of All Varieties

In Seaports of the Far East, Allister Macmillan, 1925

With the low scales of living…all manner of petty larcenies are worth while. Pieces of zinc are torn from hoardings and sold for the equivalent of threepence, ricksha fares at night have their hats snatched from their heads. Confidence tricks are also ingenious. A familiar one is to entrust the victim (usually a woman) with a "roll of notes" to be changed, and as an afterthought to demand some security against her bolting with the money. Only after the swindler has disappeared does the dupe discover that she has parted with her ring or other jewelry in return for a roll of waste paper. Another fraud is known as "flying the white pigeon." Therein the matchmaker, for a consideration, finds a concubine for the victim, which the young lady remains a while, and then disappears to repeat the swindle elsewhere.

The Chinese craving for offspring is an encouragement to kidnappers, and abductions for ransom also occur in Hongkong as in China, the captives being taken into China, sometimes tortured and killed and part of the body returned to the relatives. More frequent and disconcerting are the armed robberies, which have necessitated strict laws and possession of arms. One of the most sensational incidents of that character in the history of the colony occurred in 1918. A gang whose lodging was being raided opened fire on the police, killing two European, an Indian, and two Chinese officers. The house was surrounded, and the scene was a repetition of the famous Sydney Street siege in London. Two of the gang were killed and one brought to justice. He was acquitted, only to be extradited by the Canton authorities and executed for brigandage in China. The smuggling of opium is another activity that provides work for a numerous preventive staff, the police, co-operating. As much as nine tons of the drug, valued at $500,000, was seized in a smuggler's cave. The poppy is still grown in China, and the "dope running" into Hongkong is a sad commentary on China's personal efforts to rid herself of the curse.

The Chinese mania for secret societies adds materially to police work. The famous Triad Society, an association of desperate criminals, was only suppressed after long effort, and periodically attempts are made to revive it.

The first step towards lightening

The White Man's Burden

is through teaching the virtues of cleanliness.

Pears' Soap

is a potent factor in brightening the dark corners of the earth as civilization advances, while amongst the cultured of all nations it holds the highest place—it is the ideal toilet soap.

Admiral Dewey (above) visited Hong Kong in 1897 while advancing America's own colonial efforts in the Philippines.

The Other Side of the Coin

I. Epstein's "Hongkong: Past and Present" in the Far Eastern Survey, *1946*

It is indisputable that the port has grown, under British administration, from nothingness to a powerful material and trading position. But its political life is dominated by a few thousand British and its economy by the British Hongkong and Shanghai Banking Corporation and such giant firms as Jardine's. Although they form ninety-nine percent of the population, the position of the Chinese has been symbolized by their exclusion from the choicest residential section – the famous and beautiful "Peak."

The colony possesses a reasonable facsimile of modern administration. But its citizens have no political rights and do not vote. An opium monopoly existed before the war, under official control but a reminder of the trade that precipitated the first Anglo-Chinese war. There is protection for life and limb, but the police, whom the people fear because they have no control over them, are corrupt.

The skyline on either side of the harbor is imposingly punctuated by the great Hongkong and Shanghai Bank Building, the palatial Hongkong, Gloucester, and Peninsula hotels and the mansions of Chinese millionaires which present an opulent and modern façade. In striking contrast to these are the brothels of Wanchai, stretching for many blocks, and the incredible slums of the western area where the crowding and tuberculosis rate are among the worst in the world. "Cockloft," "cubicle" and "bed-space" are the commonest terms in Hongkong's housing vocabulary. The "cubicle" – ten feet or so square – is often the home of a family of six. Tens of thousands of homeless "street sleepers" have been a municipal problem for many years, without perceptible improvement.

Morrison Street, 1910s.

The Star of Hong Kong

The Star Ferry Company, originally the Kowloon Ferry Company, was founded in 1888 by Parsee merchant Dorabjee Nowrojee as a four "Star" fleet: *Morning Star, Evening Star, Rising Star* and *Guiding Star*. Before the Star Ferry, most trips between Hong Kong and Kowloon side were made by sampan, or in later years motor-driven boats known as wallah-wallahs. Now that the journey was quick and painless, thousands rode the Star Ferry daily. For many years, foreigners wishing to ride on the upper deck were required to dress properly and paid 15 cents for the privilege compared to one cent for the lower berth. It is still in service today as both a popular mode of transport and tourist attraction.

Ill-starred Ferries

From E.J. Eitel's Europe in China, *1895*

One instance of Chinese enterprise was the attempt made in July 1873, to run steam ferries between Hong Kong and Kowloon City, though the movement was stopped at the time through the action of the British consul in Canton, who represented to the viceroy that the ferry boats were merely intended to bring customers from Hong Kong to the Kowloon gambling houses.

Where East Meets West

Excerpt from The Critic in the Orient *by George Hamilton Fitch, 1913*

Queen's road, the main business street of Hongkong, furnishes an extraordinary spectacle at any hour of the day. The roadway is lined with shops, while the sidewalks, covered by the verandas of the second stories of the buildings, form a virtual arcade. These shops are mainly designed to catch the eye of the foreigner, and they are filled with a remarkable collection of silks, linens, ivories, carvings and other articles that appeal to the American because of the skilled labor that has been expended upon them. Carvings and embroidery that represent the work of months are sold at such low prices as to make one marvel how anyone can afford to produce them even in this land of cheap living.

Here East and West meet in daily association. The Englishman is easily recognized by his air of proprietorship, although his usual high color is somewhat reduced by the climate. He has stamped his personality on Hongkong and he has built here for generations to come. The German is liberally represented, and old Hongkong residents bewail the fact that every year sees a larger number of Emperor William's subjects intent on wresting trade from the British. Frenchmen and other Europeans pass along this Queen's road, and the American tourist is in evidence, intent on seeing all the sights as well as securing the best bargains from the shopkeepers. All these foreigners have modified their garb to suit the

Queen's Road Central, 1910s.

Queen's Road West, 1880s.

climate. They wear suits of white linen or pongee with soft shirts, and the solar topi, or pith helmet, which is a necessity in summer and a great comfort at other seasons…All the Orient is represented by interesting types. Here are rich Chinese merchants going by in private chairs, with bearers in handsome silk livery; Parsees from Bombay, with skins almost as black as those of the American negro; natives of other parts of India in their characteristic dress and their varying turbans; Sikh policemen, tall, powerful men, who have a lordly walk and who beat and kick the Chinese chair coolies and rickshaw men when they prove too insistent or rapacious; Chinese of all classes, from the prosperous merchant to the wretched coolie whose prominent ribs show how near he lives to actual starvation in this overcrowded land; workmen of all kinds, many bearing their tools, and swarms of peddlers and vendors of food, crying their wares, with scores of children, many of whom lead blind beggars. Everywhere is the noise of many people shouting lustily, the cries of chair coolies warning the passersby to clear the way for their illustrious patrons.

The Chinese seem unable to do anything without an enormous expenditure of talk and noise. Ordinary bargaining looks like the beginning of a fierce fight. Any trifling accident attracts a great crowd, which becomes excited at the slightest provocation. It is easy to see from an ordinary walk in this Hongkong street how panic or rage may convert the stolid Chinese into a deadly maniac, who will stop at no outburst of violence, no atrocity, that will serve to wreak his hatred of the foreigner.

The Hong Kong Parsee Cemetary, Happy Valley.

Parsees

Parsees – Indian Zoroastrians of Iranian descent – were one of the smallest communities in old Hong Kong, but one of the most significant contributors to its development. In the early years, the colony did the majority of its banking through India, a lucrative opening for Parsee bankers, who later helped plan the Hongkong and Shanghai Banking Corporation. It was a Parsee cook turned businessman, Dorbjee Naorojee, who created what would become the Star Ferry Company in 1888 and the 1911 donation by Parsee merchant Sir H.N. Mody of HK$180,000 helped to establish Hong Kong University. Parsees were also noted philanthropists in the area of public health, with the Ruttunjee family name connected with several hospitals.

Yet their prominence and generosity was not always enough to overcome the city's sharp racial divisions. Parsees were excluded from many local organizations and even the local theatre, but were able to mingle with their European counterparts freely at the race course, of which many were avid supporters. As the banking industry gradually shifted into British hands, the Parsee community's prominence and population trailed off, but the remains of many of their early notables can still be found at Hong Kong's Parsee Cemetery in Happy Valley.

Sir Hormusjee Naorojee Mody

G.H. Bateson Wright, Headmaster of Queen's College, in Twentieth Century Impressions of Hongkong, Shanghai, and other Treaty Ports of China, *1908*

Mr. H.N. Mody…comes of a well-known Parsee family, is one of the oldest residents, and one of the most striking personalities in financial circles, in Hongkong. It is more than forty-seven years since he came to the Colony to enter the service of a firm of Hindoo bankers and opium merchants. With them he remained for three years before launching his own opium business, which rapidly grew to large dimensions… Refusing to recognise the existence of such a word as " impossible " he soon came to the front, and for years he has played the leading part on the local stock exchange, carrying through many transactions of considerable magnitude. More than once he lost his all, for in his career he has had difficulties to overcome and obstacles to surmount, but with fine courage and estimable self-confidence he has braved the storms and steered his barque to safety. Always possessed of a marvellous memory and a wonderful fund of energy and zeal, even now, at an age when most business men are content to rest on their laurels, his activity is proverbial… Numerous and varied as are Mr. Mody's business interests, however, he still finds time to take

a prominent part in social life. Many charitable institutions have benefited considerably by his munificence, and though he carries on his good work in a quiet unostentatious manner, his benevolence and public spirit are gratefully recognised by the community…On several occasions he has won the local Derby as well as other important races. Mr. Mody brings to the turf that integrity and steadfastness of purpose which have served him so well in business, and the enthusiastic manner in which his many victories have been acclaimed testifies unmistakably to the high place he occupies in the public esteem. His hospitality, too, is renowned and, among all nationalities, he is recognised as a prince of good fellows.

The *NEW BUICK* is the *NEW STYLE*

A triumph in individual beauty … a refreshing and radical departure *from* the tiresome commonplace … a new style, a richer style, a more alluring style than the world has ever known!

The Dragon Motor Car Co., Ltd.
Telephone Central 1246 or 1247.
33, WONG NEI CHUNG ROAD, HAPPY VALLEY.
WHEN BETTER AUTOMOBILES ARE BUILT   BUICK WILL BUILD THEM.

107

The Peak

Victoria Peak, also known as Taiping Mountain or more commonly 'The Peak', was both socially and geographically as high as one could go on Hong Kong Island. Blessed with cool, breezy weather in the oppressive summer months, it was a most pleasant retreat from the sweaty bustle below. Governor MacDonnell turned a defunct sanatorium on the Peak into his residence, Mountain Lodge, in 1867 and others were followed suit. Before long, the Peak was littered with the ostentatious mansions of high colonial officials and Taipans.

Getting to the Peak was no easy matter in those days. Its steep and laborious paths were often staked out by bandits. These problems were solved in 1888 with the opening of the Peak Tram, but before this, European residents would hire coolies to carry them up in sedan chairs, costing about 1¢ an hour for two coolies or 8¢ for four coolies.

A symbol of British colonial snobbery, the Peak was strictly off limits to Chinese and Eurasians except, of course, servants. Few non-British could have afforded it in the early 20th century, but the ordinance prohibiting them from doing so was deeply resented and a rallying point for anti-imperialists. Some Chinese were allowed to move to the Peak in the 1930s, but the ordinance was not officially repealed until 1946.

Moving on Up

From the 1881 journal of the sons of the Prince of Wales, Albert and George
Looking eastward along the ridge from Victoria Peak to Mount Gough we were much surprised to find what a number of merchants' houses – we can count more than 50, each with its lawn-tennis court and racket court – have been built up there, on what a short time ago was a barren hill top with nothing but scrub and heather. There are admirable roads, and telephone and telegraphic communication with the town below, and they are talking of making a wire tramway up and down.

Latitudinal Laziness

From Round the World *by Scottish-born American steel magnate Andrew Carnegie, Dec. 14, 1878*

It is the thing in Hong Kong to do the Peak, and we did it, but not in a manner very creditable to our staying powers, I fear. The fact is, we had been tossed for sortie days upon a small ship. It was exceedingly warm. We were very tired (conscience suggested another word for tired); in short, there were a dozen reasons — good, bad, and indifferent — why two strong, lusty fellows should, under the circumstances, be carried up instead of attacking the Peak on foot; and so each of us, in a sedan chair, borne by four strong coolies, managed to get to the top and enjoy the splendid view, coming down in the same novel manner. It was surprising, after we had returned, to find how decided a misunderstanding had arisen between us on the subject. I had not pressed walking up on Vandy's account, while he had only denied himself that wished-for pleasure in deference to my supposed inability. You see, had this point been made clearer before we started, we might have had the walk after all. As it is, the credit of both is fairly maintained, and I do think that neither of us regrets the unfortunate misunderstanding; one gets so lazy in these latitudes!

"Why, the people here live in palaces!"

Governor William des Voeux, 1880s

The Opium War

The English began their battle for free trade in China back with the fruitless Macartney Embassy in 1793, followed by the even less successful Amherst Embassy (1816). By 1834, the Crown was losing its patience and Chief Superintendent of Trade at Canton, Lord Napier, tried to force their hand by launching gunboats up the Pearl River, but they were torn to pieces by Chinese cannons and Napier died shortly thereafter. When Commissioner Lin Tse-hsu seized British opium warehouses in Canton in 1839 (which were there illegally, mind you) and expelled the merchants, that was the final straw.

British merchants fled to Macau and then Hong Kong, but their chiefs made for London to demand intervention. The island was declared British territory on January 26, 1841, and the fighting that became the First Opium War began that spring. Before long, the Chinese were trounced by the vastly superior British Navy and the Commander of the British forces, Capt. Elliot, negotiated Hong Kong into the terms of surrender, which were rejected. Foreign Secretary Palmerstone rebuked the decision to claim such a worthless piece of land and had Elliot replaced with Sir Pottinger, but he also broke rank and snuck in Hong Kong.

The infamous Treaty of Nanking, signed on 29 August, forced the Chinese to repay them $6 million in lost opium revenues, open five 'Treaty Ports' to foreign trade (the most famous being Shanghai) and cede the island of Hong Kong to the Crown indefinitely (not leased as is often believed, that was for Kowloon and the New Territories much later). Whether they wanted it or not – and most did not – the British now had their strategic base in China.

French cartoon from around the time of the First Opium War.

"There can be neither safety nor honour for either government until Her Majesty's flag flies on the coasts in a secure position."
Capt. Elliot, 6 April 1839

"Why should the rebellious barbarians be allowed to keep it permanently?"
Ch'i-ying, Imperial negotiator of the Treaty of Nanking, 1842

Arid, Malarial Rock

O.M. Green's "Great Britain and Japan's War on China" in Pacific Affairs, *1938*

Hongkong, at that time an arid, malarial rock, was also ceded to Great Britain. It has been conjectured that the mandarins who signed the Treaty had but the vaguest idea of where Hongkong was. Neither side had any conception of the immense importance it was to attain; indeed there were many angry questions in Parliament as to what the use of the place could ever be.

Hong Kong, 1845.

British troops preparing for the Japanese invasion, 1941.

Protected and Controlled

Sir Henry Lord Pottinger, 1842

[T]he retention of Hong Kong is the only single point in which I intentionally exceeded my modified instructions, but every single hour I have passed in this superb country has convinced me of the necessity and desirability of our possessing such a settlement as an emporium for our trade and a place from which Her Majesty's subjects in China may be alike protected and controlled.

111

The Scandalous Force

From The British Empire Series Vol. I *by Dr. James Cantlie, 1899*

The force on shore is made up of about 100 Europeans, 100 Indians (Sikhs so called), and 300 Chinese. At the present moment there is considerable scandal in connection with the acceptance of bribes by the European police, and men of great local experience are being got rid of because they took "tips"; surely a well-understood purloin of the police in all countries. The "Sikh" policemen are voluntary recruits from different parts of India; but the majority do not belong to this warlike tribe, but to a caste of a lower order. They are endowed with a keen sense of usury, and this may be said to be their only drawback as efficient police. The Chinese members, if not quite reliable as regards their moral tone as police, are invaluable aids in the detection of crime.

Race Riots

An excerpt from John Stuart Thomson's The Chinese, *1909, describing a large-scale Chinese-Sikh confrontation*

The thick turbans of the Indians saved their heads, but many Chinese skulls were fractured. Amusing scenes were presented, a thin, tall Indian grasping a Chinese by the pig-tail, while the stout Chinese was reciprocating by the equally gross insult of unwinding the Indian's red turban.

SIKH UT ANTE

"A.S.O.P. [Assistant Superintendent of Police] (loq.) Now you understand? You may always shoot a Chinaman." From The China Punch *in 1867.*

Marked Men

The following ordinance was passed by Gov. Davis in 1845, though Triads – a secret criminal society – would go on to have a long and prosperous history in Hong Kong
Whereas the Triad Society and other secret societies prevalent in China exist among the inhabitants of the island of Hongkong, and whereas these associations have objects in view which are incompatible with the maintenance of good order and constituted authority, and with the security of life and property, and afford by means of a secret agency increased facilities for the commission of crime and for the escape of offenders…if any person or persons being of Chinese origin in the said island or its dependencies shall be a member or members of the Triad Society or other secret societies as aforesaid, he she or they shall in consequence thereof be guilty of felony, and being duly convicted thereof shall be imprisoned for any term not exceeding three years, with or without hard labour, and at the expiration of such term of imprisonment, that such person shall be marked on the right cheek in the manner usual in the case of military deserters and be expelled from the said island.

The Great Hong Kong Typhoon

In Hong Kong, typhoons can appear suddenly and wreak great havoc on the harbour and surrounding areas. The cost to old Hong Kong was substantial in both property and lives. In the following passage from My Life in China *(2007), William Elmgreen describes one of the most deadly typhoons in Hong Kong's history.*

During the night of terror in Hong Kong, between the 1st and 2nd September 1937, I was eyewitness to the deadliest and most destructive storm experienced by the Royal Observatory there…The loss of life from the typhoon was terrifying. Of 3,500 junks and sailing craft, 1,250 were sunk and 600 seriously damaged. There was the loss of 11,000 lives, maximum wind velocity 192 mph, 167 nautical mph or 307 km/hr, the highest recorded then…Of 101 large steam vessels berthed in Hong Kong Harbour and its environs, 28 were stranded on the rocks around the periphery…Why then did 28 large vessels break away from their moorings and land on the rocks when they were so securely tied up? The explanation is simple enough: a chain's strength is no greater than its weakest link. If only one boat was not suitably tied up and did tear away from its moorings, it would be blown across the harbour at fantastic speed, colliding with ships on the way, breaking their moorings and they, in turn, would be transformed into speeding 'missiles', wreaking havoc in their paths and completing their destructive work.

A Hong Kong stamp from the period of Japanese occupation 1941-1945.

114

Wreckage and Desolation

From J.S. Thomson's Straits of Malacca, Indo China and China, *1875*

In Hongkong the wind with a sudden blast has riven away the corners of houses, and sent projecting verandahs flying across the streets...The sky was of dark leaden colour...the heavy stone-faced wall of the Praya had given way, and the great granite blocks of which it was composed had been washed in upon the road...the tops of the waves were caught up by the tempest in its fury and hurled in blinding spray into, and even over the houses. We had to cling to the lamposts and stanchions, and to seek shelter against the doorways and walls...Next morning the whole length of the Praya presented a scene of wreckage and desolation. Many of the Chinese, notwithstanding their shrewdness in predicting storms, had been taken quite unawares, and hence the fearful sacrifice of life and the loss of property which had ensued.

The Great Error

An early visitor to Hong Kong, midshipman Frank S. Marryat, describing his opinion of the young colony in his travel book Borneo and the Indian Archipelago, *1848.*

Society is in a queer state here, as may be imagined when I state, that the ship-owner won't associate with the small merchant, and the latter will not deign to acknowledge a man who keeps a store. Under these circumstances, the army and navy keep aloof, and associate with no class. There were very few ladies at Hong Kong at this time, and of what class they were composed of may be imagined, when I state that a shopkeeper's sister was the belle of the place, and received all the homage of the marriageable men of Hong Kong. Hospitality to strangers is as yet unknown, and a letter of introduction is only good for one tiffin, or more rarely one dinner. I made several excursions to the country, but did not find any thing worth narrating, or describing with the pencil.

It is here worthy of remark, that there is every prospect of all the enormous expense which has been bestowed upon this island being totally thrown away...that in a few years Hong Kong will be totally deserted, and all the money expended upon it will be lost...The great error of the last war was, our selection for such an unhealthy and barren island as Hong Kong as our pied-à-terre in China...

Murders and robberies were of daily, or, rather, nightly occurrence at Hong Kong, the offenders being Chinese, who are the most daring robbers perhaps in the world.

A self-portrait by George Chinnery.

"Chinnery is supposed to be the greatest of Eastern painters…I read in a certain Indian journal the description of some scenery which was said to be "worthy of the pen of a Byron and the pencil of a Chinnery," a juxta-position of names which rather astonishes an Englishman."

A field officer in The Last Year in China to the Peace of Nanking, *1843*

117

The Governors

There were undoubtedly far more desirable diplomatic postings in the Empire than governor of old Hong Kong. Trying to please the Foreign Office, foreign merchants and Chinese working class at the same time was nearly impossible, and between the crime, corruption, diseases and natural disasters, there was always something to be blamed for. Most were unfamiliar with Hong Kong's problems and were shipped out just as they began to learn.

Governor J.F. Davis, for example, dismissed a popular chief justice and was so despised that no one attended the normally popular Governor's Cup horse race that year and, when he left, only his staff said goodbye. Governor J.P. Hennessey tried to provide more opportunities to the colony's Chinese residents by offering government jobs and opening the library to them, which made him a hero of the Chinese (whose population jumped by about 50% during his tenure) but aroused the ire of the Europeans and got him shipped off to Mauritius. A decade later, Governor William Robinson revoked funding for all schools unless they taught the English language, which pleased the merchants but was apparently not popular with higher powers: his reign saw the devastating drop of the dollar, the death of the Hong Kong cricket team at sea, two massive typhoons and an outbreak of plague.

A good job it was not, but the terms were short (most governors served for five years or less) and, as a small consolation, you usually got a street named after you.

The Japanese would later add a tower and other additions to Government House (the Governor's residence), seen here in 1891.

"It is extraordinary – not to say discreditable – that after fifty-five years of British rule, the vast majority of Chinese in Hong Kong should remain so little anglicized."
Gov. Robinson, 1895

I Thought They'd Never Leave

"Around-the-World Letters" by
Charlotte Ehrlicher, 1913
The next day we witnessed the
departure of the Governor and
his wife from Hong Kong. It was
quite exciting. The British troops
were on parade, the band played,
and the Governor in a top hat
inspected all the Tommies and
shook hands with the officers.
His wife held a regular reception,
dressed in white, with a black
picture hat, and seated in a white
sedan chair carried by four coolies
in white. All this took place on
the water front. A little launch
was waiting, all decorated with
flowers. A gorgeous lingerie pillow
was ready on her deck chair, and
a double line of aristocratic little
Chinese children, dressed in their
very best, presented bunches of
flowers. The Chinese children
and young girls are adorable.
Everybody was surprised to find
them so beautiful. As the little
launch puffed out to the steamer,
an escort of two other little tenders
went along with baskets swinging
at the back, shooting off fire
crackers. They looked like poor
little mongrel dogs with a bunch
of fire crackers tied to their tails.
The moment the official party had
turned its back, the spick and span
coolies whipped off their white
leggings and trotted down the
street in their bare legs.

Des Vouex Street, 1910s.

119

Easy Passage

From The International Relations of the Chinese Empire, *Hosea Ballou Morse,*
1918

Hongkong is an island, as close to the mainland of China as is Staten Island
to that of New Jersey, and much closer than the Isle of Wight is to England.
The entrance to the harbor is only six hundred yards wide, and, until 1899, its
northern shore was under Chinese Jurisdiction; while all along the northern
side ships (junks or others) could slip from the security of British waters into
Chinese waters at any point with the utmost facility. Hongkong then—not only
the town of Victoria, but the whole of the 29 square miles of the island and the
two square miles of the Kowloon extension—inevitably became the centre of
an active smuggling trade.

> "There are always adventurers at Hong Kong who, for a
> price, will land any number of Remingtons and any amount of
> ammunition at lonely spots along the coast of the islands."
> *H. Irving Hancock,* Uncle Sam's Boys in the Philippines, *1912*

"The island
of Hongkong
will probably
become the
favourite
resort of the
smugglers and
debauchees of
that quarter of
the globe."
*A high British
official, 1841*

Devils of the West

From In Eastern Seas *by J.J. Smith, 1883*

It is allowed to be the most cosmopolitan city in the world. Representatives of races far in excess of the Pentecostal catalogue, may be encountered in its streets in any hour's walk; men of all shades of colour and of every religious creed live here side by side in apparent perfect harmony. The Chinese who form the bulk of the population live entirely apart from the "*Ung-moh*" (red hair devils) as they flatteringly term us. English manners and customs do not seem to have influenced the native mind in the smallest degree, in spite of our charities and schools—a fact we cannot wonder at, taking into account our *diabolical* origin.

Good as New

From In Eastern Seas *by J.J. Smith, 1883*

In the earlier days of the first occupation, the English residents of Hong Kong were often placed in difficulties about their clothing, Chinamen not having attained to that perfection in the tailors' art which they now have acquired. On one occasion an old coat was supplied to a native tailor as a guide to the construction of a new one; it so happened the old garment had a carefully mended rent in its sleeve—a circumstance the man was prompt to notice—setting to at once, with infinite pains, to make a tear of a similar size and shape in the new coat, and to re-sew it with the exact number of stitches as in the original.

Chinese sketch of an English Sailor during the First Opium War, 1839.

Hong Kong in Festal Array

From The Shipwreck *by Joseph Spillman, 1906*

The New Year came and found Hongkong in festal array. All the Chinese houses were decorated with plants and flowers, and from long cords stretched from house to house, and diagonally across the streets, were suspended hundreds upon hundreds of lanterns of various colors. At the first peep of day thousands of people, dressed in holiday attire, began to throng the streets and crowd into the great open squares, where eatables of all sorts were to be had. Here were tables loaded down with all kinds of Chinese delicacies, many of which, I fear, my little readers would not find palatable. For example, there were sugar-coated worms, preserved red snails, trepang, a kind of sea-worm, — and putrid doves' eggs in an unspeakable sauce. The cakes made of honey, sugar and rice-meal, I am sure, would have been much more to your liking. Each hour the crowd increased, as the people poured into the city from the villages on the island of Hongkong, and from neighboring places…Whenever a Chinaman met an acquaintance, putting his hands in the wide, flowing sleeves of his gown, he greeted him with many bows, wished him a happy New Year, and invited him to have a cup of tea or saki. Even the poorest people had saved up enough to take part in the celebration. All over the great city joy reigned.

A Commendable Idea

Gwen Priestwood, "Aided in Escape by Friendly Chinese Guerrillas", in The Argus *10 Feb. 1945*

After some time we set out again on foot for the next point in our journey. We had a couple of heavily armed guerrillas as escort. One of them, a fat, jolly chap, had been a bell-boy at the Peninsula Hotel in Kowloon. He said he'd quit because he'd sooner shoot Japs than wait on them. I thought this was a commendable idea.

The Peninsula Hotel, one of Hong Kong's most luxurious, was built in 1928 by Sephardic Taipan Sir Elly Kadoorie. During WWII, the Peninsula served as the headquarters of the Japanese army.

> Every Chinese going out after dark must carry a light. From 8 P.M. till morning Gunfire, any Chinese found without a Pass and light will be taken into custody. Any servant who may be sent out during the above period must be furnished with a Pass and light by his Employer.
>
> *Official notification, 1865*

Koro

An excerpt from Kevin Sinclair's memoirs, Tell Me A Story, *telling the story of how he and his journalist colleagues on* The Star *newspaper created a panic in 1960s Hong Kong over the disease, koro, which causes a victim to believe his penis is shrivelling up and disappearing.*

Suddenly, our phones went mad. Every Chinese paper in Hong Kong as well as radio talk-back shows was on the line. What, please, was koro and how did you catch it? Geoffo called Alberto and got him to look up medical encyclopaedias. Armed with expert knowledge, Dr Somers wrote the second edition lead full of little known facts about how a man's pride and joy could suddenly without warning start to dwindle and disappear...Next morning, all hell broke loose. Every Chinese paper had gone berserk. Interviews with herbalists gave startling remedies for koro. Ancient crones in decrepit brothels spoke knowingly of the ailment. Suddenly, a disease that nobody had heard of 24 hours earlier was stalking the streets of Hong Kong ready to pounce on any unsuspecting male.

One Chinese paper had sketches showing people how to tie a string around the end of the member and attach this to your belt, so if koro suddenly struck and your old fellow started to withdraw, you could haul it back...no newspaperman could resist it. Even the staid Morning Post began to cover it. Nobody could ignore it because suddenly the unknown phenomenon was very real...The more imaginative reporters held professional discussions with ladies of the evening in Wanchai seeking learned advice about how the curse could be contained.

"Bride gives Singapore love-bite cure," was the resulting headline. We ran a story saying a sure-fire cure was for a lady friend to gently bite the end of the member to prevent it shrinking and disappearing. Sure enough, next day we had a fantastic picture of two ambulance men racing a stretcher-borne victim across a pavement, his wife/girlfriend walking sideways as she bent across the stretcher applying the miraculous Singapore remedy...Geoffo recalls: "The Boss's eyes glowed. A smile of glee formed on his lips. Instantly he turned to me and – snapping his fingers impatiently – rasped, "Where's the fucking photo."

Fortune Smiles

From Dust and Foam *by T. Robinson Warren, 1859*

My first step on going ashore was to look around me and see what I could do to make the pot boil, for I had no idea of letting people know that I was, as they say in California "dead broke." Knocking around among the shipmasters, I found that there was a scarcity of officers, and that high wages were being paid to respectable men, as mates, especially for Coolie ships, of which there were a great number fitting out, bound for Australia and California. Fixing upon a pretty clipper brig as the most desirable, I made an application to the captain, and was accepted *sur le champ*, as the Frenchman have it, was paid $100 in advance, and what was best of all, was informed that my services would not be required for a fortnight, thus giving me an opportunity for seeing Macau and Canton, and enjoying myself generally. Cat-like and with my usual good luck, I had fallen upon my feet, and among good Samaritans, having taken lodgings at the City Hotel, kept upon the Americo-Anglo-Chinese plan, by one Marcus Shaw, as goodhearted a little Englishman as ever drank toddy, with spacious billiard rooms, and bowling saloons; it was the resort of the fancy of Hong-Kong, *i.e.* the army and navy officers, and shipmasters generally.

Hong Kong waterfront, 1869.

The Noonday Gun

In Hong Kong, a three-pound gun in Causeway Bay is fired every day at noon. The local legend has it that early in the colony's history, Jardine and Matheson used to fire guns to welcome their Taipans back to Hong Kong, typically a naval honour. For this gross misconduct, the Navy ruled that the firm was required to fire a noonday gun each day as punishment. In fact, time keeping in Hong Kong was generally done by naval cannons fired intermittently throughout the day until 1869. A manager at Jardines decided to keep the tradition alive and bought a gun of his own, which became the official 'noonday gun'.

Mad Dogs and Englishmen, go out in the midday sun.
The smallest Malay rabbit deplores this stupid habit.
In Hong Kong, they strike a gong, and fire off a noonday gun.
To reprimand each inmate, who's in late.
In the mangrove swamps where the python romps
  there is peace from twelve till two.
Even caribous lie down and snooze, for there's nothing else to do.
In Bengal, to move at all, is seldom if ever done,
But mad dogs and Englishmen go out in the midday sun.
Noel Coward, "Mad Dogs and Englishmen", 1932

"Hongkong has now no connection whatever with China, being entirely a British possession, and has been converted from a barren rock to a most lovely, thriving and important commercial town and naval base, and is the greatest triumph of British enterprise and material civilisation that I know of."
Oliver G. Ready, 1904

One Can Almost Forget

From The Shipwreck *by Joseph Spillman, 1910*

On the north side of the island stands the capital city, Victoria, in which tier above tier, stair-like the rows of houses and splendid buildings rise one above another up the side of a hill. Beautiful quays, broad streets lined with shade trees, churches, barracks, theaters, hospitals, hotels, and shops with great show windows take one back in thought to the European capitals; and as the elaborately decorated pagodas are not near to the Christian churches, and, as there are not many more Chinese than English people in the streets, one can almost forget that he is within the confines of China and a tropical land.

Cathedral of the Immaculate Conception.

> "The visitor does not wonder that the British coveted Hongkong, for it is one of the best harbours in the world. Certainly no other is more impressive."
>
> *Arthur Judson Brown,*
> New Forces in Old China, *1904*

Better than Expected

From Adventures of a Boy Reporter *by Harry Steele Morrison, 1900*

After a short and pleasant voyage they reached Hong Kong, and Archie found this city to be much more interesting than he had expected to find it. It was charming, he thought, to run across a place which combined the conveniences of England and America with the picturesque oddities of China and Japan, and he enjoyed himself to the utmost during the two days they spent there...They found many wonderful things to look at, and Archie said that he couldn't imagine any more delightful place[.]

All Sorts of Festivities

From Crown and Anchor *by John Conroy Hutcheson, 1896*
We all of us enjoyed our long stay at Hong Kong…for, the residents were accordingly hospitable and kind to us, including the principal merchants of the place and the government officials, as well as the military stationed at Kowloon on the mainland opposite, where there was a large camp—all of them keeping open house, where we were welcomed at all hours, dinners, balls, picnics and all sorts of festivities being the order of the day while we remained in Victoria Bay.

A reception for the Duke of Connaught at the original Hong Kong Club, 1870.

The Day of the Apocalypse

Clifford W. Collinson's Half the Seas Over, *1933*
On the last night but one of our stay in Hong-Kong there was a lunar eclipse, which created a good deal of consternation amongst the Chinese, who thought that the end of the world was at hand. And so relieved were they the next morning to find that everything was still normal, that they celebrated their deliverance by indulging in an orgy of fireworks.

128

The European Stamp

A Woman's Journey Round the World *by Ida Pfeiffer, 1852*
Victoria is not very pleasantly situated, being surrounded by barren rocks. The town itself has a European stamp upon it, so that were it not for the Chinese porters, labourers, and pedlars, a person would hardly believe he was in China. I was much struck at seeing no native women in the streets, from which it might be concluded that it was dangerous for a European female to walk about as freely as I did; but I never experienced the least insult, or heard the slightest word of abuse from the Chinese; even their curiosity was here by no means annoying.

Rotating Door

From China in Transformation *by Archibald R. Colquhoun, 1898*
The history of a place like Hongkong is a curious study. The European population is constantly changing, for foreigners remain as short a period as possible: they come to make a fortune or competency, and then return to the mother-country. It is this continual change of local leaders which makes it so difficult to trace any distinct evolution of local, as distinguished from imperial, policy. The same mistakes, the same criticisms, the same apprehensions, recur again and again; the experiences of those who have left the place being too rapidly lost sight of.

International Hong Kong?

As World War II drew towards a close, US President Franklin Roosevelt proposed that it be not returned to the British after the Japanese surrender but made an international port or handed back to the Chinese. Needless to say, the British disagreed and in August 1945 Colonial Secretary Gimson rushed out of Stanley Prison and quickly reasserted British rule. Roosevelt was succeeded by Truman, who was less keen on the idea and the issue was dropped. Hong Kong quickly recovered and prospered under British rule.

British and Nationalist China flags flying after the liberation of Hong Kong, 1945.

"Oliver Stanley, Secretary of State for the Colonies…was told by the President when visiting Washington in January 1945, 'I do not wish to be unkind or rude to the British…but in 1841 when you acquired Hong Kong, you did not do so by purchase.' To which Stanley, thinking on his feet, replied, 'Let me see, Mr President, that was about the time of the Mexican War, wasn't it.'"
Frank Welsh, A History of Hong Kong, 1993

"Your return, Sir, we hope and believe, marks a new epoch in the history of the Colony… It signifies the birth of a new Hong Kong."
Sir Man Kam Lo to returning Governor Young, 16 May 1946

The Pirate Prince of Hong Kong

Cheung Po Tsai, whose Hong Kong hideout in Stanley earned the town the name 'Bandit's Pillar' in Cantonese, was as powerful a Chinese pirate as ever set sail. The son of a Guangdong fisherman, Cheung Po was kidnapped by the pirate king Cheng I and the 'Dragon Lady of the South China Sea', Cheng I Sao (literally 'Cheng I's wife). The couple 'adopted' him, though more likely as a sexual plaything than as a son. When Cheng I died in 1807, Cheng I Sao seized command of his Red Fleet, promoted Cheung Po to no. 2 and eventually married him.

The flamboyant Cheung Po, usually adorned in purple silks and a black turban, and his Cantonese- prostitute-turned-buccaneer wife made a fearsome pair. Their fleet boasted as many as 1,000 junks and 80,000 men by some estimates. They laid down a pirate code of laws, both brutal and effective. Disobey an order, lose your head; don't share the booty, lose your head; desert, lose your ears; rape a captive, lose your head or, *if she consented*, lose your head and toss her overboard. They did no fear the imperial rulers of China and once even assassinated the Viceroy of Zhejiang. Cheung Po wasn't afraid of foreigners either, and, after being chased

off by Western gunboats, got a 24-pound cannon of his own.

But he could not outrun his enemies forever and was forced to surrender the fleet in 1810. Cheng I Sao was offered amnesty and went back to Canton, where she opened a very successful gambling house. Cheung Po couldn't be kept from the seas and rose to the rank of admiral in the Chinese navy, spending the rest of his days hunting down pirates and occasionally reverting to his old ways.

Ladder Street, 1925.

Many-coloured

From Isabella Bird's The Golden Chersonese and the Way Thither, *1883*

Victoria is a beautiful city. It reminds me of Genoa, but that most of its streets are so steep as to be impassable for wheeled vehicles, and some of them are merely grand flights of stairs, arched over by dense foliaged trees, so as to look like some tropical, colored, deep colonnades. It has covered green balconies with festoons of creepers, lofty houses, streets narrow enough to exclude much of the sun, people and costumes of all nations, processions of Portuguese priests and nuns; and all its many-colored life is seen to full advantage under this blue sky and brilliant sun.

PIRATES.—Piracies in all the waters of Kwangtung continue to be of frequent occurrence. Sometime ago a large cargo boat near the Bogue, on her way from Canton to Hongkong, was plundered of everything, but nobody on board injured. It is said that within the last three months not fewer than two hundred and nineteen cases of Piracy committed within the jurisdiction of Kwangtung have been brought under the notice of the provincial government.

When a lady elopes
Down a ladder of ropes,
She may go, she may go,
She may go to—Hongkong—for me!
A ditty recalled in My Days of Adventure
by Ernest Alfred Vizetelly, 1914

The Greatest Tailor in the World

From The Three Admirals *by W.H.G. Kingston, 1878*

Mr Tung-Cheong came forward with a smiling countenance, guessing, as he surveyed the tattered uniforms of the three midshipmen, what they required.

"Me thinkee greatest tailor in the world. Thinkee nothing to make coat'ees for three gentlemans," he observed, as he pointed to the uniforms of every possible description hanging up in the shop. He at once produced a midshipman's uniform, which he kept as a specimen to show of what he was capable, and having taken their measures, he promised that all three should be ready the following evening, together with every other article they might please to order. They, of course, wanted shirts, socks, caps, and shoes, swords and belts, all of which, to their surprise, he had in stock — indeed, he showed, like most of his countrymen, that he had a keen eye for business, and would undertake to fit out a ship's company, from an admiral down to a powder-monkey.

All Work and No Play

From Harold MacGrath's The Ragged Edge, *1902*

I can't keep a good man beyond three pay-days. They want some fun, and there isn't any. No other white people within twenty miles. I've combed Hong-Kong. They all balk because there aren't any petticoats. I won't have a beachcomber on the island. The job is easy. The big pay strikes them; but when they find there's no place to spend it, good-bye!

Jardine's Bazaar, 1950s.

"Perhaps no place in the history of ages can boast such a rapid rise as the town of Hong-kong"
Arthur Cunynghame, 1844

The bronze statue of Queen Victoria in Central, called "the Black Queen of the White British" by the Chinese. The statue was destroyed during WWII

A Question of Motives

From American Through the Spectacles of a Chinese Diplomat *by Wu Tingfang, 1914*
From an economic and moral point of view, however, I must admit that a great deal of good has been done by the British Government in Hongkong. It has provided the Chinese with an actual working model of a Western system of government which, notwithstanding many difficulties, has succeeded in transforming a barren island into a prosperous town, which is now the largest shipping port in China. The impartial administration of law and the humane treatment of criminals cannot but excite admiration and gain the confidence of the natives. If the British Government, in acquiring the desert island, had for its purpose the instruction of the natives in a modern system of government, she is to be sincerely congratulated, but it is feared that her motives were less altruistic.

"Hongkong is the ideal British crown colony, "the brightest gem in the colonial diadem" of King Edward, etc., etc., of which every Englishman is proud."
William Eleroy Curtis, 1905

134

Armoured Junks

This excerpt from The Times *shows that pirates were still a menace as late as Feb. 5, 1946*

Chinese pirates… with Japanese armament, are making territorial waters increasingly unsafe for any but reasonably well-armed shipping…In armoured junks, the pirates have even entered Hong-kong harbor. A week ago they held up the ferry from Macau to Hong-kong at the point of a machine gun, and stripped and robbed over a hundred passengers almost within sight of their homes…

British commandos are reinforcing the under-staffed water police, and the navy is using submarines, assault and landing craft, Fairmine launches, and even large vessels to fight the scourge.

The Pirate Queen

The New York Times, *Jan. 14, 1923*
"All went well on the outward passage." Mr. Webb said, "but on the trip back a band of pirates numbering about fifty, who were among the deck passengers and under the command of a woman suddenly held up all the Europeans in the first cabin at the point of a revolver and got away with about $50,000 in cash and jewelry. The two Indian guards on board who were armed with rifles, put up a fight, but they were taken by surprise and were shot and then dumped over the side. The pirates then rushed the gangway firing their revolvers as they went along the deck and very soon had the whole ship under their control…" The whole thing had been planned and carried out by the female pirate captain and under her directions the pirates stripped the Sui-An of everything they could lay their hands upon and then took the steamship to one of the islands past Hong Kong and left with their plunder in a big junk which was waiting for them.

135

An Unwelcome Influence

From The Far Eastern Tropics *by Alleyne Ireland, 1905*

It is discouraging to find that, as far as one can judge, three hundred and fifty years of contact with the white man has made no appreciable change in the Chinaman.

In talking over the matter with one or two highly educated and widely traveled Chinese gentlemen in Hong Kong, I was told that, with the exception of a mere handful of men in Hong Kong and the Treaty ports, contact with Western civilization had absolutely failed to change a single trait in the Chinese character; that we are as much hated and despised as ever we were by the mass of the people ; that as far as the present is concerned, the existence of powerful armed forces alone insures the lives of the foreigners ; and that, for the future, the probabilities pointed to the total exclusion of the foreigners from China. This they all deplored; but it was their sincere conviction.

> "Englishmen have evidently forgotten, or would like to forget, how they got that ideal piece of property."
> *William Eleroy Curtis,* Egypt, Burma and British Malaysia, *1905*

Cornflakes with Chopsticks

In Hongkong China *from the U.S. Navy Ports of the World series, 1921*
Since Hongkong is near the tropics and the native dress is more suitable for warm weather than European clothing, the action of many of the natives in donning Western garb constitutes an appeal obviously to vanity rather than comfort...Another Western "custom" which has acquired favor in the native quarter of Hongkong is that of eating cornflakes, and the practice has caused the Chinese as much trouble and discomfort as that of wearing European clothing. One writer remarks that the first Chinese to eat cornflakes with chopsticks deserves special commendation for patient endeavor.

"Passing westward along Queen's Road we come upon a quarter of the town much frequented by seamen of all nations. Here spirits are sold in nearly every second shop and bands of common sailors may be seen...roaring out some rough sea-song in drunken chorus[.]"
J.S. Thomson, The Straits of Malacca, Indo China and China, *1875*

A Good Time

James Cantlie, The British Empire Series, *1899*
Life in Hong-kong is by no means the exile to Europeans that its distance from Europe and civilisation generally might imply. The British, with that aptitude in adapting themselves to surroundings which characterises them in every part of the world, manage to have what our American cousins would call a "good time."

The Value of Life

From My Colonial Service *by Gov. William Des Vœux, 1903*

I was told that before the Government instituted a reward for life-saving it not uncommonly happened that when a sampan was upset, the occupants of other boats passing made no efforts to save from drowning the people thrown into the water, but calmly allowed them to perish. This indifference is, however, by no means solely with regard to the lives of others. For, as is well known, when a man is condemned to death, it is by no means difficult to procure a substitute who is willing to undergo execution himself on condition that provision is made for his family.

"His one remaining resource was a Canadian Pacific steamer from Victoria. This, he figured out, would get him to Hong Kong even earlier than the steamer which he had already missed. He had a hunch that Hong Kong was the port he wanted. Just why, he could not explain."
Arthur Stringer, Never-Fail Blake, *1913*

An Eye-sore to Native Pride

In Rev. George Smith's Consular Cities of China, *1847*

The lowest dregs of native society flock to the British Settlement, in the hope of gain or plunder. Although a few of the better classes of shopkeepers are beginning to settle in the colony, the great majority of the new comers are of the lowest condition and character...At Canton the greatest unwillingness exists in the minds of respectable natives to incur the odium which attaches to any connexion with Hong Kong. It is not unnatural that such a prejudice should exist in the minds of the patriotic Chinese against a settlement wrested from them by the sword; and that the Chinese rulers should invest with the utmost degree of odium a locality which must be a continual eye-sore to their pride.

On its Head

In Foot-prints of Travel *by Maturin M. Ballou, 1888*

These streets exhibit strange local pictures. The shoemaker plies his trade in the open thoroughfare; cooking is going on at all hours in the gutters beside the roads; itinerant pedlers dispense food made of mysterious materials; the barber shaves his customer upon the sidewalk; the universal fan is carried by the men, and not by the women. The Chinese mariner's compass does not point to the North Pole, but to the South; that is, the index is placed upon the opposite end of the needle. When Chinamen meet each other upon the streets, instead of shaking each other's hands they shake their own. The men wear skirts, and the women wear pantaloons. The dressmakers are not women, but men. In reading a book a Chinaman begins at the end and reads backwards. We uncover the head as a mark of respect; they take off their shoes for the same purpose, but keep their heads covered. We shave the face; they shave the head and eyebrows. At dinner we begin the meal with soup and fish; they reverse the order and begin with the dessert. The old men fly kites while the boys look on; shuttlecock is their favorite game; it is played, however, not with the hands, but with the feet. White constitutes the mourning color, and black is the wedding hue. The women perform the men's work, and the men wash the clothing. We pay our physicians for attending us in illness; they pay their doctors to keep them well, and stop their remuneration when they are ill. In short, this people seem to be our antipodes in customs as well as being so geographically.

Chinese artist in Hong Kong, as captured by John 'China' Thomson in 1868.

"I am groping in the mists of Chinese physics and metaphysics, a shape like the ghost of Aristotle or Plato rising up ever anon before me. I go to grasp it — and a Chinese folio interposes its knotty pages."

Hong Kong protestant missionary
James Legge, 1849

"There life rolls by, varied, swift, happy, useful. After three or four years one goes to recuperate in Old England. After fifteen or twenty years one retires there. One goes home wealthy. One is looked up to by reason of this hard earned wealth; and thereafter attentive and indulgent one follows and encourages the efforts of those who, in their turn, strive and strain to conduct on so high a plane, with such faith and indomitable energy, the destinies of the Anglo-Saxon race."

J. Chailley-Bert, La colonisation de l'Indo-Chine, *1894*

Health Before Wealth

Letter from A RESIDENT in China and the Chinese, by Henry Charles Sirr, 1849
The strong man and the weak, the sober man and the drunkard, the man who never exposed himself to the sun, he who defied it – all died alike: the healthy man, the woman, and the infant withered under the poison of Hong-Kong fever with equal rapidity. If any man, therefore, have a mind to visit China, from curiosity, let him turn his time and his money to better account. If any man be allured to it by the love of gain, let him think that health is better than wealth; and if any unfortunate individual in either of her Majesty's services be compelled to come, by duty, just let him have a stout heart and "a lively faith in God's mercy," which latter may spare him to curse the place, as it has done the writer of these few lines; and if, after his term of service here, he leaves it for a more hospitable shore, after having escaped fevers and typhoons, he may say and think to himself, "that verily Providence has watched over him."

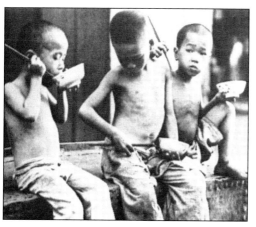

> "Vice must be pretty much the same all the round world over, but if a man wishes to get out of pleasure with it, let him go to Hong-Kong."
> *Rudyard Kipling, 1899*

Fast Society

In Due West by Maturin Murray Ballou, 1884
Society in the city is entirely English, and, to use an expressive word, is "fast." Balls, races, regattas, and fêtes of all kinds follow each other with ceaseless energy. The gayety of domestic and social life, and the luxurious mode of living generally, exceed that of any European colony we have chanced to meet with. Club life, evening entertainments, and late hours, are the characteristics of Hong Kong; the serious affairs of life seem to have been left at home in far-off England, – an inevitable result where the military element enters so largely into the community.

141

Dr. Hong

An excerpt from Tutt and Mr. Tutt *by Arthur Train, 1920*

Now he—Mr. Tutt—had an interpreter, the well-known Dr. Hong Su, against whom nothing could be said, and upon whose fat head rested no imputation of partiality; a graduate of Harvard, a writer of note, a—

O'Brien sprang to his feet: "My interpreter says your interpreter is an opium smuggler, that he murdered his aunt in Hong Kong, that he isn't a doctor at all, and that he never graduated from anything except a chop-suey joint," he interjected.

"This is outrageous!" cried Mr. Tutt, palpably shocked at such language.

The Wicked Vegetable

An article from the 1878 China Mail, *describing the kudzu root*

There is a vegetable much eaten by the Cantonese which goes by the name of kot. In Hong Kong and other places where foreigners are to be found the proper word kot is seldom used, but, instead of it, the apparently awkward expression shat sam ngau. The reason for this is that kot is considered to be an unlucky sound, and like such syllables as sz, kau, &c. is tabued as often as possible from familiar conversation. Many natives will be found quite unable to give any satisfactory reason for tabuing this word, but occasionally one will be found who can give the true one, which is this: kot is a very wicked word in the foreign languages, and when joined to the word tam or the word mai (i. e., God d--, or my God), signifies something very terrible connected with the spirits or persons of your ancestors (which by the Chinese are greatly feared), and is generally accompanied by a ferocious look on the part of the imprecating foreigner, and, possibly, a box on the ear at the same time. Let not philologists lose sight of such facts as these when searching for their whys and wherefores.

Inferno at the Derby

It was a grim day at the 1918 Hong Kong Derby, the colony's most beloved horse racing event, when a fire killed almost 600 people. The races were wildly popular with the Chinese, who were not at that time allowed into the European seating area, so a makeshift bamboo and palm-leaf grandstand had been erected for them. The structure was unfit to support the huge crowds that came for the derby and it collapsed onto the flames of the snack vendors underneath. A mass panic ensued in which hundreds of Chinese were incinerated, trampled or suffocated. For years after the fire, the memory of the massive death toll kept many Chinese spectators from returning, fearing the vengeful spirits of the deceased.

TRAGEDY AT HONGKONG.

600 LIVES LOST.

SOME FRIGHTFUL SCENES.

A Mind-mouldering Time

Albert Smith's To China and Back, *1859*
The young men in the...large Houses have a sad, mind-mouldering time of it. Tea-tasting, considered as an occupation, does not call for any great employment of the intellect, and I never saw one of the young clerks with a book in his hand. They loaf about the balconies of their houses, or lie in long bamboo chairs, smoke a great deal, play billiards at the Club, where the click of the ball never ceased from the earliest morning, and glance over the local papers. These journals are mostly filled with the most uninteresting, incomprehensible and infinitesimally unimportant local squabbles...

Queen's and Prince's Buildings, 1910s.

A Delightful Winter

Constance Cumming, 1878
Another week has glided by, and each day convinces me more and more that it would be simply impossible to find more delightful winter-quarters. Morning, noon, evening and night are all beautiful and all pleasant, and there is the delight of continuous fine weather, which is warranted to continue throughout the five winter months...And the human life is equally characteristic. There is a very large, agreeable European society – naval, military and civil – with surroundings of quaint Chinese men and women-the former with their long plaits, the latter with wonderfully dressed glossy hair. Judging from my own experience, I can never again pity any one who is sent to Hong Kong – at least, in winter.

144

Purse-proud Stuck-up-ism

Henry T. Ellis' Hong Kong to Manilla, *1859*
The English residents at Hong Kong, like many other small communities, were divided by exclusive feelings, which rendered society far less agreeable than it might have been had a better understanding existed among them…The most absurd part of this purse-proud stuck-up-ism, was that with the exception of a few Government employés, they were all more or less rowing in the same boat, i.e., striving to amass as many dollars as opportunity would admit of; and though some were called merchants, and others storekeepers, such was the undercurrent of retail speculation, that it was hard to define where one batch ended and the other began.

The Office in Charge,

  No. 2, Police Station,

  (或改寫 The *Public Dispensary, Central District.*)

Dear Sir,

  I beg to bring to your notice that there is a dead body lying on the road (或改寫 *pathway*) in front of my house (或改寫 *of house No. 24, Mercer Street.*) It is apparently that of a male person (或改寫 *of a child*) who the Kaifong people think has died of some sickness.

  The Kaifong will be extremely obliged by your sending an ambulance to remove it to the proper quarter.

  Apologizing for the trouble given:

            Yours faithfully,

                  Chan Che Wing

"Europeans in Hongkong live in a very expensive style; much more expensively, one would think, than they need do, when we consider that many of the necessaries of life are to be had at prices very little in advance of our market rates at home."
        J.S. Thomson, The Straits of Malacca, Indo China and China, 1875

The Peak Hotel early 1900s.

Ho Kai

Sir Kai Ho Kai was the most respected Chinese in Hong Kong in his day. Born the son of a Chinese protestant pastor in 1859, Ho Kai received a bilingual education in Hong Kong before becoming the second Chinese to study in England, where he received degrees in medicine and the law. Hard though it may be to imagine in colonial Victorian society, he courted and married an Englishwoman, Alice. She died soon after the couple returned to Hong Kong, and Ho Kai founded the Alice Memorial Hospital in her memory.

Ho Kai was a man of many talents. He was a Justice of the Peace, a member of the sanitary board and the first permanent Chinese member of the Legislative council, holding the latter two posts a record 24 years. Though an active mason, one of the first Chinese to adopt Western dress in Hong Kong and a loyal British subject, Ho Kai was also fiercely devoted to the modernization of China. He inspired and later conspired with his medical student, Dr. Sun Yat-sen, in his plans to overthrow the Qing Dynasty.

Ho Kai was also involved in numerous property dealings in Kowloon and the New Territories. It is his later partnership with the business mogul Au Tak, beginning in 1912, that he is best remembered for. Together they bought a large strip of reclaimed waterfront land in Kowloon and immodestly called it the 'Kai Tak Bund'. The investment, like many of Ho Kai's business decisions, was a disaster. When he died in 1914, he left behind 17 children, his second wife and a mountain of debt. The Kai Tak Bund was eventually reclaimed by the government in 1924 and turned into Kai Tak Airport, the only thing in the former Colony that bore his name until it was closed in 1998.

> "Among the Chinese there are many who have profited by a thoroughly sound and high-class European education, but there are few who have had a more distinguished academical career, or have used their advantages to better purpose than Dr. Ho Kai."
> *Twentieth Century Impressions of Hong-Kong, Shanghai, and Other Treaty Ports of China, 1908*

A Man of Vision

Count Hermann Keyserling, The Travel Diary of a Philosopher, *1925*
I feel this evening as I look from the Peak upon the expanse of the Chinese Sea as if new forces had been born in me: I perceive delicacies and shades in colour and form which I missed altogether a few days ago…I see it already: in China I will have to transform myself into a man of vision; here all appearance seethes with significance. There looms, before my mind's eye, a synthesis of essence and semblance such as I have never met with before.

> "[H]e carried away no immediate personal impression, beyond a vague jumble, in the background of consciousness, of Buddhist temples and British red-jackets, of stately parks and granite buildings, of mixed nationalities and native theaters, of anchored warships and a floating city of houseboats."
> *Arthur Stringer,* Never-Fail Blake, *1913*

Kai Tak Airport, seen here in 1946, was created in 1925 for a flight school that failed after a botched-parachute-landing-turned-drowning marred its opening ceremony. It was used privately by the Hong Kong Flight Club and, from 1936, as a commercial airport. During the Japanese occupation, two additional runways were built using forced labour, and the Sung Wong Toi, a monument to the last Song Emperor who died nearby, was destroyed in the process.

Peacekeepers

Captain George Younghusband on leave from India in 1894, from On Short Leave to Japan, *1894*
"We don't want any of your soldiers here – the fleet is enough for us," said a leading merchant to me. Of course, he knew best. Later, at dinner, I happened to ask why all the troops were garrisoned in the close, hot town, instead of on the airy and salubrious Peak. "Bless you, there are 200,000 Chinamen in this town to be kept in order!" said the same member.

Marsh Road, Wanchai 1950s.

"I cannot well avoid adding one word on the vexed question of the immense Chinese population in Hong-Kong; there are certainly the elements of great mischief in case of any rising, but danger there is none…for the men-of-war of all nations…would be fully equal to cope with any emergency: they could blow up all Hong-Kong in a few hours[.]"

Captain S.H. Jones-Parry, My Journey Round the World, *1881*

Vegetating in Office

From Tales of Men and Ghost *by Edith Wharton, 1910*

Oh, nothing became of him—because he became nothing. There could be no question of 'becoming' about it. He vegetated in an office, I believe, and finally got a clerkship in a consulate, and married drearily in China. I saw him once in Hong Kong, years afterward. He was fat and hadn't shaved. I was told he drank. He didn't recognize me.

"One of the peculiar difficulties against which this Government has to struggle is the enormous influence wielded by the great and opulent commercial houses against whose power and in opposition to whose personal views it is hard to contend."

Gov. Bowring, 1850s

A reproduction of the first sketch of Hong Kong by Clark Abel in 1816, featuring the Pokfulam waterfall.

"At the upper end of the sea is Hong Kong, a hot, unhealthy, and disagreeable island, but which gives her what she wants, a depot and a base from which to threaten and control the neighboring waters. Clearly the Chinese Sea, the artery of Oriental commerce, belongs far more to England than to the races which border it."

The Atlantic Monthly, *July 1863*

Taking to the Streets

Strikes, common in Hong Kong almost from its establishment, often brought business to a standstill and served as a visible reminder of just how much the colony depended on its cheap, abundant labour force. Though most strikes were in response to laws deemed unfair, the coolie strikes of 1895 were in response to plague-prevention sanitation measures and an example of the deep distrust that existed between the colonized and colonizers. As the years progressed, labour strikes took on an increasingly anti-foreign tone and small sparks could ignite a massive revolt. Such was the case of the 1922 Seaman Union's strike, which quickly grew from 30,000 to 120,000, including most of the Chinese workers in Hong Kong. Martial law was instituted and when many strikers attempted to leave for Guangdong on March 3, a guard at Sha Tin opened fire, killing three and injuring several more. The anti-foreign strikes in 1925 (the 'May 30th Movement') that engulfed southern China, dealt a massive blow to Hong Kong shipping, which declined more than half during the peak of the protests. By June 30, the protest grew to such proportions that the Hong Kong Volunteer Corp was required to put it down, but boycotts of Japanese and British goods lasted until October of the next year.

> "Years ago, all coolies doffed their caps and stood on one side; now they don't..."
> *Granville Sharp, 1895*

Chinese Strike Ties Up Hongkong.

VANCOUVER, B. C., March 1.—The strike of Chinese seamen which has crippled commerce in the Far East and especially at Hong Kong, has assumed more serious proportions, a cable from Hong Kong received today said. Overnight, according to the message, the strike became general, involving a general tie-up. The port has been closed and land transportation practically suspended. It is estimated that the monetary loss already is $40,000,000.

A Coming Storm

From Magnus Hirschfeld's Curious Sex Customs in the Far East, *1935*

[I]n Hongkong a European merchant told me with a laugh that a Chinese sedan-chair coolie (by the sweat of their brow they carry the people who lie on the heights up hill and down dale) had once said to him that if he were born again he would like to be the dog of a rich Englishman; "they have it good," added the firm believer in the transmigration of souls. "How can you laugh about it?" I replied to the man who told me of it. "It's a tragic story."

The antagonism of the Chinese soul toward the foreigner cropped out in its most elementary form a generation ago in the Boxer Rebellion and to a lesser extent three years ago in the Hongkong coolie strike (when one morning all the foreigners found themselves without service). It flames up now here, now there, in delirious shootings (at many street crossings in Shanghai and elsewhere one sees wire barricades, guarded by policemen, in readiness at any moment to bar the way to the Chinese). It seems to me to be the light before a perhaps not very distant world storm.

A State of Panic

Sir Henry Pollock to departing Gov. Clementi, Jan. 28, 1930

In the summer of 1925, labour trouble broke out with the fierceness of a tempestuous sea. The Communists took advantage of the situation to create disturbance, as a raging fire is fanned, or an agitated sea is lashed by the wind. The markets and marts were in a state of panic. Many forsook their occupations and migrated elsewhere. In those critical days, the bond between Hongkong and Canton, which are to each other as lips are to the teeth, was sustained as by a fraying thread.

Kowloon Mosque, early 1900s.

Capable Barbarians

From The Shipwreck *by Joseph Spillman, 1910*
"The barbarians of the West are a capable people after their fashion," said Lohe. "See what a great city they have built here where a few years ago there were only a half dozen or more bamboo huts. And, too, each day their power increases…"

Victoria Theatre, early 1900s.

Scandalous Attire

From Things Chinese *by J. Dyer Ball, 1903*
White is never seen as an outer garment on women in Canton or Hongkong, except to please Europeans; this colour being reserved alone for undergarments, in which, of course, a woman would be ashamed to appear in public.

Opium (Divans) (No. i).-The Prepared Opium Ordinance, 1897, required opium divans to be licensed by the Colonial Secretary. The present Ordinance enlarges the definition of an opium divan. Regulations for the management of such opium divans are made (March 1st, 1898); among others, the licensed keeper is to provide two photographs of himself for identification.

The Journal of the Society of Comparative Legislation, 1899

Completely Inconsistent

James Lafayette Hutchison in China Hand, *1936*

British Hongkong must be the tidiest of all the tidy cities of the world, and the most completely inconsistent. It looked in the early morning as if overnight a corps of efficient charwomen had given it a thorough sweeping. Even the foliage of the undergrowth and trees softening the contours of the hills seemed to have been dusted and polished to silvery high-lights against the vivid green. And like good boys and girls, the foreign element went to bed at 10 o'clock, at which hour everything closed by law. Yet the Chinese shops on the sides of the stone steps at the bottom of the hills were brown with dust and smelled to heaven. And the night life among the native residents was only starting at midnight and was about as free and unmoral as in New York during prohibition.

Kowloon City, early 1900s.

A Curious Mixture of Contradictions

James Lafayette Hutchison in China Hand, *1936*

Some one had told me the day before that the English imposed a fine for taking off one's coat in public – even on the hottest day. I thought of all the formal cleanliness I had seen, of the 10 o'clock curfew, then of the tremendous racket going around me and the open consumption of opium. What a curious mixture of contradictions the Englishman is – morality as such plays no part in his life – he is ruled by the one and only law of "it's done or it isn't done".

The Coolie

A poem in The Drum-Wave Island and Other Verses *by B. N., 1904*

Round his head his hair is coiled
In a coarse cloth turban-wise,
His dress is ragged and badly soiled
And bloodshot are his eyes.
His jacket, open, displays his chest
A full deep copper-brown–
This fellow, pig-tailed Chinaman'
Of Nursery renown.

He wouldn't answer a call of 'John,'
He eats no dogs or mice,
The best of the food he lives upon
Is rice, and always rice;
He doesn't 'savvy' the pigeon-talk
That we always thought was due
From every pig-tailed Chinaman
Of brightest yellow hue!

He is not child-like, he is not bland,
He wears no guileless smile,
And, if we really could understand,
His words are often vile;
But he works all right, and he carries loads
That would break a dray-horse down–
This Chinaman 'with the almond-eyes'
Of Nursery renown.

"What are coolies as distinguished from other Chinese? They are what we call at home "common laborers"… They are just muscle. They are born to toil, to carry burdens, to pull rickshaws, to do the menial work, to bear without alleviation the Primal Curse."
F. Dumont Smith, 1907

God Only Knows

A letter by Charles Richard Thomas, 14 August 1937
Out in the streets China carries on. The old men sit on the pavements smoking their long pipes and philosophically regarding the passers by, the women cook their rice on the small fires in the gutters and the children in amazing numbers play their queer card games. Soon the chopsticks will come out, the families will squat round in circles and China will eat her last meal of the day. Afterwards they will stretch out their mats and sleep impervious to the patter of feet by them and the rattle of the buses and tramcars in the roadway. God only knows what life holds for these people!

The Hughesiliers

Despite all being over 55 years old and with some up in their seventies, the 'Hughesiliers' (after their commander, Hughes) showed the Japanese they still had plenty of fight left in them. On December 19, 1941, the 72 men held the advancing Japanese column at bay at the Hong Kong power plant. Despite being outmanned and outgunned by a presumably much younger opponent, they did not cede their ground or surrender until they were out of bullets. And rather than go peaceably, they opted to fight their way out, losing several brave elderly gentlemen in the process.

Japanese bombers striking Hong Kong, Dec. 1941.

"I had no illusions about the fate of Hong Kong under the overwhelming impact of Japanese power. But the finer the British resistance the better for all."
Winston Churchill, The Second World War, Vol. 3, *1950*

The Praya

The Praya, Hong Kong's waterfront, was created and expanded through ambitious 'land reclamation' projects, which artificially expanded the coastline. The idea was first conceived of in 1855, but not carried out until 1868 and again in 1890, adding about 60-65 acres. Many of the colony's most important buildings like the Hong Kong Club and the Prince's Building are now located on the Praya. In the following excerpt from An American Cruiser in the East, *John D. Ford describes the Praya in 1898.*

The Praya, the road along the bay-front, extends from the parade to the extreme northwest end of the town, and is lined with fine shops and storehouses, while its roadway is crowded

with busy men and women. The Queen's Road is lined on both sides with fine shops, filled with beautiful and rare wares from every part of China, Japan, India, and Africa. Silks, crapes, gauzes, cabinets, ivories, lacquers, porcelains, precious stones, rare filigree in gold and silver, and cunning work in camel's hair and fine wools, are lavishly displayed to tempt the traveller; and the roadway swarms with a motley crowd of Europeans, Jews, Japanese, Koreans, Mahometans, Hindoos, Malays,

Javanese, Parsees, Sikhs, Cingalese, Negroes, half-castes, and everywhere that unfortunate Chinese coolie, — the drudge, the bearer of the world's loads and burdens.

The "Sikh" policeman, in dark blue, with immense scarlet turban, stands "attention" at the corner of the road. White-robed "ayahs" and Koreans stride from shop to shop, while the pedlers cry their wares. Everybody is talking in this great Babel. "Tommy Atkins," the high private, with cap on ear and switch in hand, swaggers up the road, the observed of all observers. A picturesque group of little musümes from "Dai Nippon" chaperone Chinese and Hindoo maidens through the mazy road. Parsees, Chinese, and Koreans discuss money, stocks, and the latest rumors from Seoul. The Turk and the Javanese hold a hot discussion. The childlike and bland Cingalese unfolds his pack, and displays beautiful emeralds, moonstones, cat's-eyes, sapphires, and diamonds that are worth a king's ransom, but can be purchased for a few shillings; and the small boys in pigtails toss the shuttlecock with knee, heel, and elbow.

Plenty Too Much Fool-o

From English Life in China *by Major Henry Knollys, 1885*

The Chinese being totally unable to pronounce our English names with any proximity to accuracy, it is customary for a visitor, even though well known, to send up his card in advance, and it is quite allowable during the hot siesta hours for the 'boy' to bring back the message 'no can see.' 'Here is that stupid Mr. Smith,' says the lady to her husband. 'Oh, do not let the snob in,' is the drowsy reply. Accordingly the 'boy' thus delivers himself to the self-complacent Smith: 'No can see. Master say you snob. Missus-ee say you plenty too much fool-o.'

"The English are aware that, while the Chinese would accomplish nothing without them, on the other hand they themselves would accomplish nothing without the Chinese: they are mutually necessary."
Archibald R. Colquhoun,
China in Transformation,
1898

Sexual Slavery

The selling of women and girls – as wives, house servants and prostitutes – was prevalent throughout old China and still persists in some regions. In Hong Kong, where criminality was abundant and women scarce, the practice of sexual slavery flourished. An estimated 18,000 women were victims in the colony by 1910, many owned by former slaves. Many of the brothel-owners were able to operate without interference from, and often with the protection of, the Colonial elite. In one telling instance, a Catholic girls' school was nearly closed in 1867, when the authorities learned that most of the girls were becoming the mistresses of European businessmen following graduation.

Stone Nullah Lane in Wanchai, 1910s.

A Life of Shame

From Fighting the Traffic in Young Girls, *Ernest A. Bell, 1910*

Traffic in Chinese girls for wicked uses extended to Hong Kong as soon as the island became prosperous and populous after being ceded to Great Britain in 1841…The system of Chinese brothel slavery differs from the white slave trade, in that the Chinese brothel slaves are not weak or wicked women who have fallen into the clutches of traffickers, as so many of our European and American white slaves unquestionably are, but are good girls who have been sold by their actual owners into a life of shame for money, sometimes sold by their own parents. Some are not sold outright, but are mortgaged to pay off a loan.

'Protected' Women

From Heathen Slaves and Christian Rulers *by Elizabeth Wheeler Andrew and Katharine Caroline Bushnell, 1907*

When once a man enters the service of Satan he is generally pressed along into it to lengths he did not at first intend to go. So it proved in the case of many foreigners at Hong Kong. The foreigner extended his "protection" to a native mistress. That "protected woman" extended his name as "protector" over the inmates of her secret brothel; and into that house protected largely from official interference, purchased and kidnaped girls were introduced and reared for the trade in women...It was sufficient for the "protected" woman to say, when the officer of the law rapped at her door, "This is not a brothel, but the private family residence of Mr. So-and-So," naming some foreigner, — perhaps a high-placed official, — and the officer's search would proceed no further.

Causeway Bay, early 1900s.

Below the Polished Surface

Hong Kong Chief Justice John Smale, Oct. 20, 1879

I fear that a high premium is obtained by persons who kidnap girls in the high prices which they realize on sale to foreigners as kept women...No one can walk through some of the bye-streets in this Colony without seeing well dressed China girls in great numbers whose occupations are self-proclaimed, or pass those streets, or go into the schools of this Colony, without counting beautiful children by the hundred whose Eurasian origin is self-declared... The more I penetrate below the polished surface of our civilization the more convinced am I that the broad under-current of life here is more like that in the Southern States of America when slavery was dominant, than it resembles the all pervading civilization of England.

"I am practically down and out myself...All I want is to get to Hongkong in peace for the April races."

Harold MacGrath, Parrot & Co., *1913*

The grandstand at Happy Valley race course around the turn of the century.

"It is said, on absolutely no foundation, that a man proposed to his lady and she turned him down. When she accepted it was in what then became Happy Valley. I told this to Brenda and she asked how the Peak got named."

Gareth Powell

It Thrills Me

From Gigolo *by Edna Ferber, 1921*

"And settle down in Okoochee! Never see anything! Stuck in this God-forsaken hole! This drab, dull, oil-soaked village! When there are wonderful people, wonderful places, colour, romance, beauty! Damascus! Mandalay! Singapore! Hongkong!...Hongkong! It sounds like a temple bell. It thrills me."

"Over in Hongkong," said Arnold Hatch, "I expect some Chinese Maxine Pardee would say, Okoochee! It sounds like an Indian war drum. It thrills me.'"

The Top Seed

From Things Chinese *by J. Dyer Ball, 1903*

[A] very common gambling amusement, and one often seen on the streets, is staking on the number of seeds in an orange. If a number of Chinese are seen surrounding a fruit hawker's stock of oranges in Hongkong, it will generally be found that this form of gambling is the attraction. Each player has a good look at the orange, a loose-skinned one, and makes a guess at the number of seeds in it, staking his money accordingly. After all have staked, the fruit-dealer skins the orange and opens each division, so as to count the pips carefully. The one that guesses right wins treble the amount of his stakes, whilst the two nearest in their guesses to him each win double theirs.

An advertisement for the Luk Kwok Hotel, the inspiration for the Nam Kok Hotel in The World of Suzie Wong.

The Nam Kok Hotel

In Richard Mason's, *The World of Suzie Wong, 1957*

The Nam Kok was not technically a brothel, for brothels were illegal in Hong Kong, and it made its profits only from the rooms, which were sometimes let several times over in the course of twenty-four hours. The girls lived outside, made their own prices with the sailors, and kept what they earned, but they provided the hotel with its life-blood, in the form of occupants for the rooms, and the bar was placed at their disposal as a hunting ground, on the condition that they did not take their pick-ups elsewhere.

"Hongkong is one of the best cities in the Orient in which to purchase supplies of almost any kind, for not only is the selection excellent, but the best English goods can be had for prices very little in excess of those in London itself."
Roy and Yvette Andrews, 1918

Philanthropy

Augustus Lindley in Ti-ping Tien-kwoh, *1866*
A couple of philanthropists one night thought to relieve me of the burden of my purse while I was taking a moonlight stroll barely beyond the houses of Victoria; but the arguments of a Penang lawyer proved so effectual…that they were glad to forego their unwelcome attentions and decamp, leaving a memento of the meeting in the shape of an ugly-looking rusty knife.

Hong Kong harbor, 1925

Me from Hong Kong

From an 1880s American folk song
Oh, my name Hay Sing, come from China,
Me likee Irish girl, she likee me.
Me from Hong Kong, Melican man come along,
Steal an Irish girl from a poor Chinee.

"Hong Kong is the great competitor, and as it has risen to the third seaport in the world's commerce, it is a formidable rival."
Robert Dollar, 1912

Inconsistent

From American Through the Spectacles of a Chinese Diplomat *by Wu Tingfang, 1914*
Once a Chinese was arrested by the police in Hongkong for cruelty to a rat. It appeared that the rat had committed great havoc in his household, stealing and damaging various articles of food; when at last it was caught the man nailed its feet to a board, as a warning to other rats. For this he was brought before the English Magistrate, who imposed a penalty of ten dollars. He was astonished, and pleaded that the rat deserved death, on account of the serious havoc committed in his house. The Magistrate told him that he ought to have instantly killed the rat, and not to have tortured it. The amazed offender paid his fine, but murmured that he did not see the justice of the British Court in not allowing him to punish the rat as he chose, while foreigners in China were allowed the privilege of shooting innocent birds without molestation. I must confess, people are not always consistent.

Hong Kong around the turn of the 20th century.

The Cosmopolitan East

In Hongkong China *from the U.S. Navy Ports of the World series, 1921*
Hongkong represents the cosmopolitan East almost as truly as New York
represents the cosmopolitan West, and the tourist finds a bewildering variety
of races on which to feast his eyes and a surprising assortment of languages
with which to deafen his ears when he lands in the port and wanders
through the city of the Fragrant Streams and Good Harbor.

"Hong Kong is,
indeed, a most
romantic spot, and
said to be the finest
harbor in the world."
Henrietta Shuck,
first female American
missionary in China,
Aug. 4, 1849

A Beautiful Woman

Laurence Oliphant, Narrative of the Earl of
Elgin's Mission to China, *1859*
It was provoking that a place possessing
so many scenic attractions should have
been so entirely devoid of charms. Like
a beautiful woman with a bad temper,
Hong Kong claimed our admiration
while it repelled our advances.

Order Out of Chaos

Sun Yat-sen, speaking to Hong Kong University, Feb. 1923
More than thirty years ago I was studying in Hong Kong and spent a
great deal of spare time in walking the streets of the Colony. Hong Kong
impressed me a great deal, because there was orderly calm and because there
was artistic work being done without interruption. I went to my home in
Heungshan twice a year and immediately noticed the difference. There was
disorder instead of order, insecurity instead of security…Afterwards I saw
the outside world, and I began to wonder how it was that foreigners, that
Englishmen could do such things as they had done, for example, with the
barren rock of Hong Kong, within 70 or 80 years, while China, in 4,000 years,
had no place like Hong Kong.

The Chinese Has It

F. Dumont Smith, Blue Waters and Green and The Far East Today, *1907*
"Better is a good name than great riches." The Chinese has it. He is no
fool; he is just as acute, as far-seeing, just as shrewd at a bargain, and
he has more honesty than any of the people who deal with him; and
there he holds an advantage. In the long run he will get his own again.
He is recovering his own trade, and he will retake Hong Kong and
Shanghai some day as he has retaken Macao.

And You?

From the letters of Anton Chekhov, 1890
The first foreign port we reached
was Hong Kong. It is an exquisite
bay. The traffic on the sea was such
as I had never seen before even in
pictures; excellent roads, trams, a
railway to the mountains, a museum,
botanical gardens; wherever you
look you see the tenderest solicitude
on the part of the English for the
men in their service; there is even
a club for the sailors. I went about
in a jinrickshaw — that is, carried by
men — bought all sorts of rubbish
of the Chinese, and was moved to
indignation at hearing my Russian
fellow-travellers abuse the English
for exploiting the natives. I thought:
Yes, the English exploit the Chinese,
the Sepoys, the Hindoos, but they
do give them roads, aqueducts,
museums, Christianity, and what do
you give them?

The old Hong Kong Post Office around 1910.

Here is Civilization!

In W. Hastings Macaulay's Kathay: A
Cruise in the China Seas, *1852*
The settlement on it was called
Victoria, but is generally known by
the name of Hong-Kong; in fact,
I believe you would puzzle some
persons if you should call it by the
former name.
Here the merchants are princes, and
dwell in princely edifices; here is
life in the streets, and people move
about as if they had an object, and
the stranger says at once, "Ah! here
is civilisation!"

Hong Kong early 20th century.

A City en Fête

H.A. Cartwright in Twentieth Century Impressions of Hongkong, Shanghai, and other Treaty Ports of China, *1908*

Viewed from the harbour, Hongkong presents a very picturesque appearance, not unlike that of the north coast of Devon, or the west coast of Scotland. At night time the scene resembles a city *en fête*. The riding lights of the shipping sparkling like gems on the bosom of the deep, the bright illuminations of the water-front, and the countless lamps that bespangle the hillsides and stretch along the terraces as though in festoons, furnish a sight that fascinates the eye and leaves an enduring impression of delight upon the mind.

Hong Kong skyline, 1950s.

Face to Face

In Hong Kong, 1862-1919 Years of Discretion *by Geoffrey Robley Sayer, 1939*

It is as the point of impact of the scientific West upon the philosophical East, of military Europe upon civilian China, that Hong Kong claims our real interest. Here – at her own doorstep – China, and hereafter traversing half the world – England, abruptly confront their antitheses. Here two peoples, each profoundly confident of its own superiority, meet face to face. The onlooker, stepping back a pace or two, watches the reaction of the one upon the other with curiosity, and not without a smile.

A Chinaman, unless he is closely watched, will keep pigs in the fourth story of a house in which perhaps a dozen families live beneath him; and on that fourth story, with its open-work floors, the pig will live and move and have his being until he changes his Saxon name for his French one.

Alleyne Ireland, 1905

The Lion and the Lamb

From Dust and Foam *by T. Robinson Warren, 1859*

The lion and the lamb lay down together. Under the very shadows of the fleet of men-of-war stationed here for no other purpose in the world than to exterminate the pirates, lay scores of junks, whose sole and only business in the world is to rob the weaker, though ostensibly engaged in fishing. Being heavily armed, they hunt down and pillage all other craft not so strong as they are. They are not so particular about the flag, but show equal favors to all. Their own countrymen they have a weakness for; but their bloodthirsty ferocity is more particularly excited when brought in contact with the Fanqui, or foreigner. Not content with robbing, they torture and murder all who fall in their power. It seems an impossibility to exterminate them, for so numerous are they, that although hundreds are yearly destroyed, thousands of others are ready to take their places. In the harbor of Hong-Kong itself, under the very guns of the frigates, vessels have been boarded and pillaged without exciting a suspicion of what was going on.

Ships in Hong Kong harbour around the 1860s.

Business as Usual

"The Anatomy of Hongkong", E. Stuart Kirby in the 1949 Far Eastern Survey
Questions as wide as the fate of Asia and the world can hardly be covered
in this short note. Hongkong people wonder a great deal about them,
but do not talk very much. Enterprisers and trouble-shooters that they
are, they get on with their business, sensing that no world–red, white, or
bloodshot–can do without Hongkong. If they had a slogan it might be
"Business as usual."

Hong Kong, 1950s.

"Hong Kong is
the greatest city
in Asia...Whoever
masters it will
eventually master
Asia."

James Clavell
Nobel House
1981

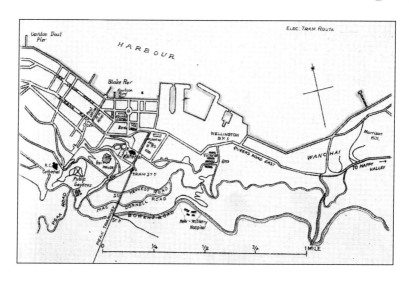

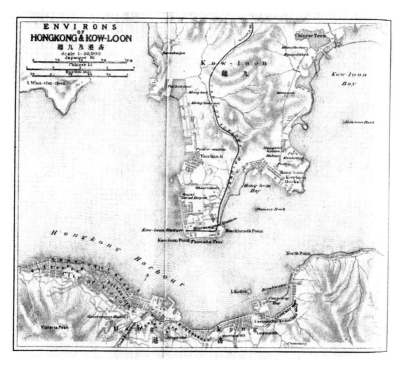

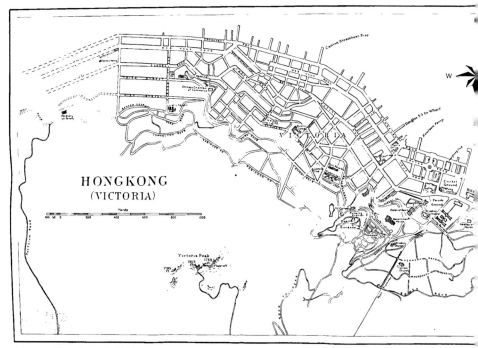

A map of Hong Kong in 1921.

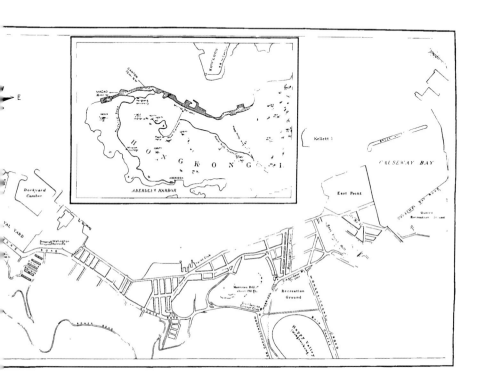

Bibliography

Abel, Clarke, *Narrative of a Journey to the Interior of China*. London: Longman, Hurst, Rees, Orme, and Brown, 1818.
Andrew, Elizabeth Wheeler, and Bushnell, Katharine Caroline, *Heathen Slaves and Christian Rulers* (1907). *Project Gutenberg*. 5 July 2004 (accessed 1 Jan. 2009. http://www.gutenberg.org/cache/epub/12818/pg12818.html.utf8).
Andrews, Roy and Yvette, *Camps and Trails in China*. New York: D. Appleton and Co., 1918.
A'Rabbitt, Shamus, *China Coast Ballads* (1938). Republished in *China Rhymes*. Hong Kong: Earnshaw Books, 2009.
"Armoured Pirate Junks". *The Times* (London), Feb. 5, 1946.
Baines, J.A., "The Population of the British Empire". *Journal of the Royal Statistical Society*, Vol. 69, No. 2 (Jun. 1906), pp. 440-443.
Ball, B.L., *Rambles in Eastern Asia*. Boston: James French and Co., 1856.
Ball, J. Dyer, *Things Chinese*. Hong Kong: Kelly & Walsh, 1903.
Ballantyne, R.M., *Under the Waves*. London: J. Nisbet & Co., 1876.
Ballou, Maturin M., *Due West*. Boston: Houghton, Mifflin and Co., 1884.
Ballou, Maturin M., *Foot-prints of Travel*. Boston: Ginn & Co., 1888.
Belcher, Sir Edward, *Narrative of a Voyage round the World performed in H.M.S. Sulphur, 1836-1842*. London: Henry Colburn, 1843.
Bell, Ernest A., *Fighting the Traffic in Young Girls*. Chicago: G.S. Ball, 1910.
Bird, Isabella, *The Golden Chersonese and the Way Thither*. New York: G.P. Putnam's Sons, 1883.
Blue, A.D., "Piracy on the China Coast". *Journal of the Hong Kong Branch of the Royal Asiatic Society*, Vol. V (1965).
B.N., The *Drum-Wave Island and Other Verses*. Hong Kong: Kelly & Walsh, Ltd., 1904.
Brando, Marlon, and Cammell, Donald, *Fan-Tan*. New York: Alfred A. Knoft, 2005.
Brassey, Annie Allnut, *A Voyage in the 'Sunbeam'*. Chicago: Belford, Clarke & Co., 1881.
Cantlie, Dr. James, *The British Empire Series, Vol. I*. London: Kegan Paul, Trench, Trübner & Co. Ltd., 1899.
Carnegie, Andrew, *Round the World*. New York: Charles Scribner's Sons, 1884.
Chailley-Bert, J., and Brabant, A.B. (trans.), *The Colonisation of Indo-China*. London : Archibald Constable & Co., 1894.
Chekhov, Anton, and Garnett, Constance, *Letters of Anton Chekhov*. New York: The Macmillan Company, 1920.
"China". *The Times* (London), Sept. 1, 1857.

China Mail, May 15 and July 27, 1878.

China Punch, June 11, 1867.

Choa, Gerald H., *The Life and Times of Sir Kai Ho Kai*. Hong Kong: The Chinese University Press, 2000.

Churchill, Winston, *The Second World War, Vol. 3*. Boston: Houghton Mifflin Company, 1950.

Clavell, James, *Nobel House*. New York: Delacorte Press, 1981.

Clavell, James, *Tai-pan*. New York: Atheneum, 1966.

Coates, Austin, *China Races*. Hong Kong: Oxford University Press, 1983.

Colcord, Lincoln, *The Game of Life and Death*. New York: The Macmillan Company, 1914.

Colquhoun, Archibald R., *China in Transformation*. London: Harper & Brothers, 1898.

Colquhoun, Archibald R., *The Mastery of the Pacific*. New York: The Macmillan Company, 1902.

Collinson, Clifford W., *Half the Seas Over*. London: Hutchinson, 1933.

Criswell, Colin, *The Taipans, Hong Kong's Merchant Princes*. Hong Kong: Oxford University Press: 1981.

Crossley, E.D., "Episode in China". *Korero*, Vol. 3, No. 2, 1945.

Cunningham, Alfred, *The French in Tonkin and South China*. Hong Kong: Hong Kong Daily Press, 1902.

Cunynghame, Arthur, *An Aide-de-Camp's Recollections of Service in China*. London: Saunders and Otley, 1844.

Curtis, William Eleroy, *Egypt, Burma and British Malaysia*. Chicago: Fleming H. Revell Company, 1905.

Davidson, G.F., *Trade and Travel in the Far East*. London: Madden and Malcolm, 1846.

Davis, John Francis, *Sketches of China*. London: Charles Knight & Co., 1841.

De Quincey, Thomas, *The Uncollected Writings of Thomas de Quincey (Vol. 2)*. London: Swan Sonnenschein & Co., 1890.

Des Vœux, William, *My Colonial Service*. London: John Murray, 1903.

Dilke, Charles Wentworth, *Greater Britain*. London: Macmillan and Co., 1890.

Dollar, Robert, *The Private Diary of Robert Dollar on his Recent Visits to China*. San Francisco: Robert Dollar Company, 1912.

Donnelly, Ivon A., *Chinese Junks and Other Native Craft* (1924). Hong Kong: Earnshaw Books (reprint), 2008.

Ehrlicher, Charlotte, "Around-the-World Letters". *American Journal of Nursing*, Vol. 13, No. 4 (Jan. 1913), pp. 305-306.

Eitel, E.J., *Europe in China*. Hong Kong: Kelly & Walsh, 1895.

Elgin, Lord James, and Walrond, Theodore (ed.), *Letters and Journals of James, Eighth Earl of Elgin*. London: John Murray, 1872.

Ellis, Henry T., *Hong Kong to Manilla*. London: Smith, Elder and Co., 1859.

Elmgreen, William, and Elmgreen, John (ed.), *My Life in China. Tales of Old China*. 2007 (http://www.talesofoldchina.com/library/elmswood.php).

Emerson, Geoffrey Charles, "Behind Japanese Barbed Wire: Stanley Internment Camp, Hong Kong 1942-1945". *Journal of the Hong Kong Branch of the Royal Asiatic Society*, Vol. 17 (1977).

"English Naval Power and English Colonies". *Atlantic Monthly*, July 1863.

Epstein, I., "Hongkong: Past and Present". *Far Eastern Survey*, Vol. 15, No. 8 (Apr. 24, 1946), pp. 113-115.

Ferber, Edna, *Gigolo*. New York: Crowell Publishing Company, 1921.

Field Officer, *The Last Year in China, to the Peace of Nanking*. London: Longman, Brown, Green, and Longmans, 1843.

Fitch, George Hamilton, *The Critic in the Orient*. San Francisco: Paul Elder and Company, 1913.

Ford, Charles, "Severe Frost at Hongkong". *Nature*, Vol. XLVII (Nov. 1892-Apr. 1893), .pp. 535-536.

Ford, John D., *An American Cruiser in the East*. New York: A.S. Barnes and Company, 1898.

Foster, Mrs. Arnold, *In the Valley of the Yangtze*. London: London Missionary Society, 1899.

French, Paul, *Through the Looking Glass*. Hong Kong: Hong Kong University Press, 2009.

Gray, Albert; Ilbert, Courtenay, and Manson, Edward, "Eastern Colonies". *Journal of the Society of Comparative Legislation*, New Series, Vol. 1, No. 3 (Dec. 1899), pp. 471-475.

Green, O.M., "Great Britain and Japan's War on China". *Pacific Affairs*, Vol. 11, No. 2 (Jun. 1938), pp. 224-232.

Hancock, H. Irving, *Uncle Sam's Boys in the Philippines*. Philadelphia: Henry Altemus Company, 1912.

Hardy, Rev. E.J., *John Chinaman at Home*. London: T. Fisher Unwin, 1905.

Harris, John R. and Lindsay, Oliver, *The Battle for Hong Kong 1941-1945*. Hong Kong: Hong Kong University Press, 2005.

Herzog, Maximilian, *A Fatal Infection by a Hitherto Undescribed Chromogenic Bacterium: Bacillus Aureus Foetidus*. Manila: Bureau of Public Printing, 1904.

Hinnells, John R., *The Zoroastrian Diaspora*. Oxford: Oxford University Press, 2005.

Hirschfeld, Magnus, *Curious Sex Customs in the Far East*. New York: Grosset & Dunlap, 1935.

Holland, J.H., "Alcohol". *Bulletin of Miscellaneous Information* (Royal Gardens, Kew), Vol. 1912, No. 3, pp. 113-130.

Holmes, E. Burton, *The Burton Holmes Lectures, Vol. V*. Battle Creek: The Little-

Preston Company, 1901.

Hongkong China. Bureau of Navigation (U.S.), 1921.

"Hongkong Honours Governor". *The North-China Herald*, Jan. 28, 1930.

Hongkong Telegraph, March 8, 1915.

"How Pirate Queen Attacked Sui-an". *The New York Times*, Jan. 14, 1923.

Hughes, R.H., "Hong Kong: An Urban Study". *Geographical Journal*, Vol. 117, No. 1 (Mar. 1951), pp. 1-23.

Hughes, Richard, *Borrowed Place, Borrowed Time*. London: Andre Deutsch, 1968.

Hutcheson, John Conroy, *Crown and Anchor*. London: F.V. White & Co., 1896.

Hutchison, James Lafayette, *China Hand*. Boston: Lothrop, Lee and Shepard Company, 1936.

Ireland, Alleyne, *The Far Eastern Tropics*. Boston: Houghton, Mifflin and Company, 1905.

Johnston , A.R., "Note on the Island of Hong-Kong". *Journal of the Royal Geographical Society of London*, Vol. 14 (1844), pp. 112-117.

Jones, Margaret, "Tuberculosis, Housing and the Colonial State: Hong Kong, 1900-1950". *Modern Asian Studies*, Vol. 37, No. 3 (Jul. 2003), pp. 653-682.

Jones-Parry, Capt. S.H., *My Journey Round the World*. London: Hurst and Blackett, 1881.

Keyserling, Count Hermann and Reece, J. Holroyd, *The Travel Diary of a Philosopher* (vol. 2). New York: Harcourt, Brace, & Company, 1925.

Kingston, W.H.G., *The Three Admirals*. London: Griffith and Farran, 1878.

Kipling, Rudyard, *From Sea to Sea (Vol. 1)*. New York: Doubleday & McClure, 1899.

Kipling, Rudyard, *The Seven Seas*. Leipzig: Bernhard Tauchnitz, 1897.

Kirby, E. Stuart, "The Anatomy of Hongkong". *Far Eastern Survey*, Vol. 18, No. 10 (May 18, 1949), pp. 114-116.

Kirby, E. Stuart, "Hongkong Looks Ahead". *Pacific Affairs*, Vol. 22, No. 2 (Jun. 1949), pp. 173-178.

Knollys, Maj. Henry, *English Life in China*. London: Smith, Elder, & Co., 1885.

Lau, P.T.,"The Aims of Chinese Nationalists". *Annals of the American Academy of Political and Social Science*, Vol. 132 (Jul. 1927), pp. 72-79.

Legge, Helen Edith (ed.), *James Legge Missionary and Scholar*. London: The Religious Tract Society, 1905.

"Letters from Hong Kong and Macao". *The New Monthly Magazine and Humorist*, Part 1 (1844).

Lilius, Aleko E., *I Sailed with Chinese Pirates* (1930). Hong Kong: republished by Earnshaw Books, 2009.

Lindley, Augustus, *Ti-ping Tien-kwoh*. London: Day & Son, 1866.

Lyster, Thomas, *With Gordon in China*. London: T. Fisher Unwin, 1891.

Macaulay, W. Hastings, *Kathay: A Cruise in the China Seas*. New York: G.P. Putnam & Co., 1852.

MacGrath, Harold, *Parrot & Co.* New York: A.L. Burt Company, 1913.

MacGrath, Harold, *The Ragged Edge.* New York: Grosset & Dunlap, 1902.

Macmillan, Allister, *Seaports of the Far East.* London: W.H. & Collingridge, 1925.

Marryat, Frank S., *Borneo and the Indian Archipelago.* London: Longman, Brown, Green and Longmans, 1848.

Martin, R.M., *China.* London: James Madden, 1847.

Martin, William, and Dickes, E.W. (trans.), *Understand the Chinese.* New York: Methuen, 1934.

Mason, Richard, *The World of Suzie Wong.* London: Collin, 1957.

Maugham, W. Somerset, *On a Chinese Screen.* London: William Heinemann, 1922.

Mayers, Wm. Fred.; Dennys, N.B.; and King, Chas.; *The Treaty Ports of China and Japan.* Hong Kong: A. Shortrede and Co., 1867.

Medhurst, W.H., *China.* London: John Snow, 1838.

"Memorandum on the Trade of Hong Kong" Memorandum (Institute of Pacific Relations, American Council), Vol. 3, No. 15 (Jul. 13, 1934).

Morrison, Harry Steele, *Adventures of a Boy Reporter.* Cleveland: World Syndicate Publishing Co., 1900.

Morse, Hosea Ballou, *The International Relations of the Chinese Empire.* London: Longmans, Green and Co., 1918.

Murray, Dian H., *Pirates of the South China Coast, 1790-1810.* Palo Alto: Stanford University Press, 1987.

Norman, Henry, *The Peoples and Politics of the Far East.* New York: Charles Scribner's Sons, 1895.

Oliphant, Laurence, *Narrative of the Earl of Elgin's Mission to China.* London: William Blackwood and Sons, 1859.

Peck, Ellen Mary Hayes, *Travels in the Far East.* New York: Thomas A. Crowell & Co., 1909.

Pfeiffer, Ida, A Woman's Journey Round the World. London: Office of the Illustrated London Library, 1852.

"Politics Determine Chinese Health". *The Science News-Letter*, Vol. 15, No. 411 (Feb. 23, 1929), p. 119.

Ready, Oliver G., *Life and Sport in China.* London: Chapman & Hall, 1904.

Pryor, E.G. "The Great Plague of Hong Kong". *Journal of the Hong Kong Branch of the Royal Asiatic Society,* Vol. 15 (1975), pp. 61-70.

"Pugilism in China". *New York Times*, Dec. 31, 1911.

Shuck, Henrietta, *A Memoir of Henrietta Shuck.* Boston: Gould, Kendall, & Lincoln, 1849.

Sirr, Henry Charles, *China and the Chinese.* London: Wm. S. Orr & Co., 1849.

Smith, Albert, *To China and Back.* London: Chapman & Hall, 1859.

Smith, F. Dumont, *Blue Waters and Green and The Far East Today.* Topeka: Crane

& Company, 1907.

Smith, Rev. George, *Consular Cities of China*. London: Seeley, Burnside, & Seeley, 1847.

Smith, J.J., *In Eastern Seas*. Devonport: A.H. Swiss, 1883.

Spillman, Joseph, *The Shipwreck* (1906). St. Louis: B. Herder, 1910.

Smyth, W.H., *The Sailor's Word-Book*. London: Blackie and Son, 1867.

Stringer, Arthur, *Never-Fail Blake*. New York: McKinley, Stone & Mackinzie, 1913.

Sun Yat-sen, "Why I Became a Revolutionist". *The Hongkong Daily Press*, Feb. 20, 1923.

Taylor, Griffith, "China. Among the Hakka Tribes". *Sydney Morning Herald*, 12 Feb. 1927.

Thomson, John Stuart, *The Chinese*. Indianapolis: The Bobbs-Merrill Company, 1909.

Thomson, John Stuart, *The Straits of Malacca, Indo China and China*. New York: Harper & Brothers, 1875.

Train, Arthur, *Tutt and Mr. Tutt*. New York: Charles Scribner's Sons, 1920.

Tsang, Steve, *A Modern History of Hong Kong*. London: I.B. Tauris & Co., 2007.

Verne, Jules, *Around the World in 80 Days*. London: Sampson, Low, Marston, Low, & Searle, 1874.

Von Hochberg, Count Fritz, *An Eastern Voyage*. London: J.M. Dent & Sons, 1910.

Warner, Anne, *Susan Clegg and a Man in the House*. Boston: Little, Brown, and Company, 1907.

Warren, T. Robinson, *Dust and Foam*. New York: Charles Scribner, 1859.

Water, Dan, "Hong Kong Hongs with Long Histories and British Connections". *Journal of the* Hong Kong *Branch of the Royal Asiatic Society*, Vol. 30 (1990), pp. 219-56.

Wells, Carveth, *North of Singapore*. New York: Robert M. McBride and Company, 1940.

Welsh, Frank, *A History of Hong Kong*. London: HarperCollins, 1993.

Wharton, Edith, *Tales of Men and Ghost*. New York: Charles Scribner's Sons, 1910.

Wise, Michael, and Wise, Mun Him, *Travellers' Tales of Old Hong Kong and the South China Coast*. Singapore: Times Books International, 1996.

Wood, James (ed.), *The Nuttall Encyclopædia*. 1907.

Worcester, G.R.G. , *The Floating Population in China*. Hong Kong: Vetch and Lee, 1970.

Wright, Arnold (ed.), *Twentieth Century Impressions of Hongkong, Shanghai, and other Treaty Ports of China*. London: Lloyd's Greater Britain Publishing Company, 1908.

Wu Tingfang, *American Through the Spectacles of a Chinese Diplomat* (1914). *Project Gutenberg*. 5 July 2004 (accessed 1 Jan. 2009. http://www.gutenberg.org/files/609/609-h/609-h.htm).

Young, Walter H., *A Merry Banker in the Far East*. London: John Lane, 1916.

Younghusband, Capt. George, *On Short Leave to Japan*. London: Sampson, Low, Marston & Company, 1894.

Yung Wing, *My Life in China and America* (1909). Hong Kong: Republished by Earnshaw Books, 2008.